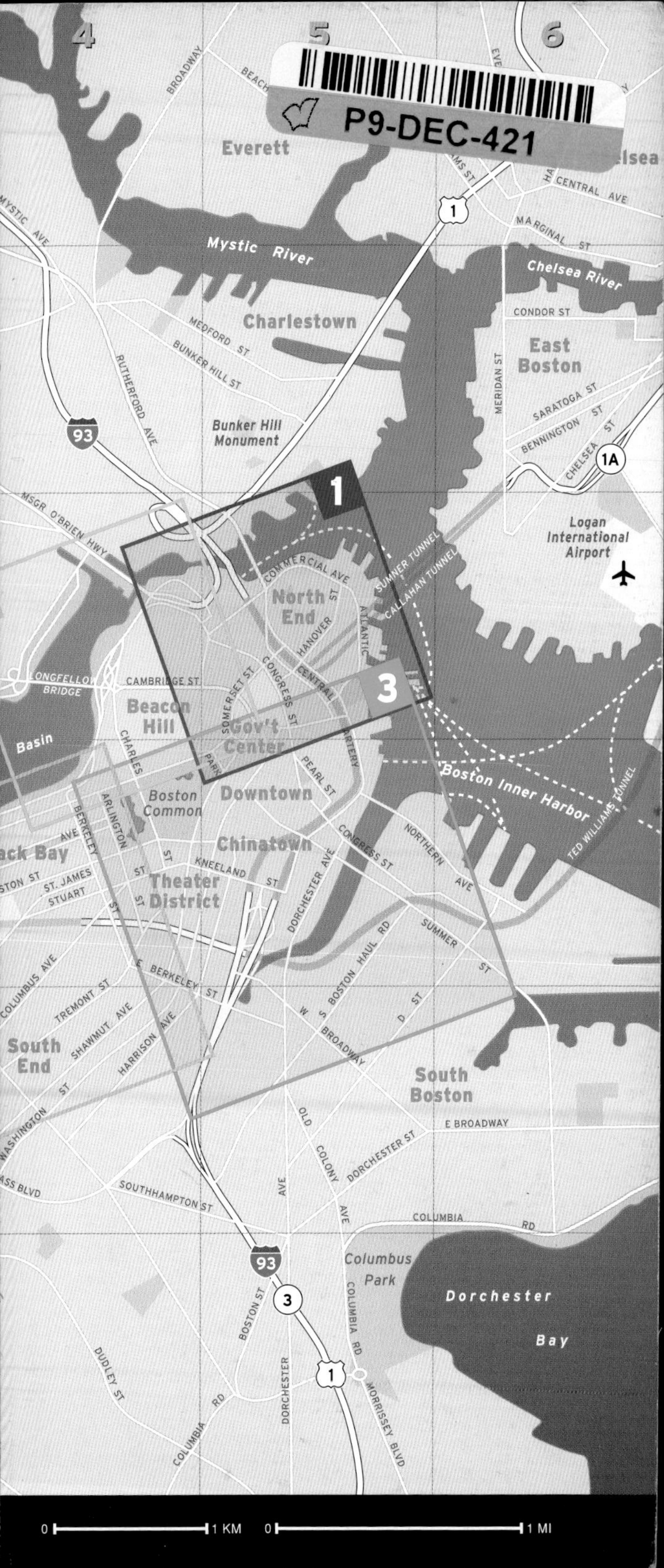
4
5
6
P9-DEC-421
Everett
Mystic River
Chelsea River
Charlestown
East Boston
Bunker Hill Monument
Logan International Airport
North End
Beacon Hill
Gov't Center
Downtown
Boston Common
Chinatown
Back Bay
Theater District
South End
South Boston
Columbus Park
Dorchester Bay
Boston Inner Harbor
Basin
LONGFELLOW BRIDGE
BROADWAY
BEACH
MYSTIC AVE
MEDFORD ST
BUNKER HILL ST
RUTHERFORD AVE
MSGR O'BRIEN HWY
CENTRAL AVE
MARGINAL ST
CONDOR ST
MERIDAN ST
SARATOGA ST
BENNINGTON ST
CHELSEA ST
SUMNER TUNNEL
CALLAHAN TUNNEL
TED WILLIAMS TUNNEL
COMMERCIAL AVE
HANOVER ST
ATLANTIC
CAMBRIDGE ST
SOMERSET ST
CONGRESS ST
CENTRAL
ARTERY
PARK
PEARL ST
CHARLES
ARLINGTON
BERKELEY
KNEELAND ST
DORCHESTER AVE
NORTHERN AVE
SUMMER ST
ST. JAMES
STUART
COLUMBUS AVE
TREMONT ST
SHAWMUT AVE
HARRISON AVE
WASHINGTON ST
E BERKELEY ST
W S BOSTON HAUL RD
BROADWAY
D ST
E BROADWAY
OLD COLONY AVE
DORCHESTER ST
MASS BLVD
SOUTHHAMPTON ST
COLUMBIA RD
BOSTON ST
COLUMBIA RD
MORRISSEY BLVD
DUDLEY ST
DORCHESTER AVE
93
1
1A
3
0
1 KM
0
1 MI

CONTENTS

BOSTON

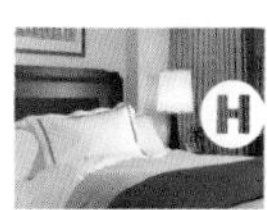

HOW TO USE THIS BOOK

MAP SECTION

- We've divided Boston into six distinct areas. Each area has been assigned a color, used on the map itself and in easy-to-spot map number indicators throughout the listings.
- The maps show the location of every listing in the book, using the icon that indicates what type of listing it is (sight, restaurant, etc.) and the listing's locator number.
- The coordinates (in color) indicate the specific grid that the listing is located in. The black number is the listing's locator number. The page number directs you to the listing's full description.

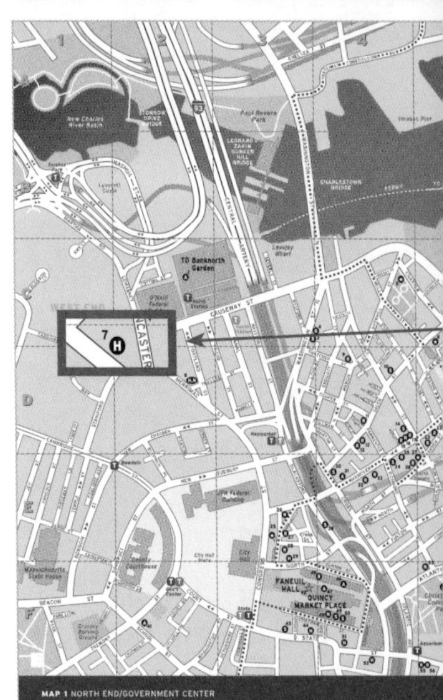

LISTINGS SECTION

- Listings are organized into six sections:
  - SIGHTS
  - RESTAURANTS
  - NIGHTLIFE
  - SHOPS
  - ARTS AND LEISURE
  - HOTELS
- Within each section, listings are organized by which map they are located in, then in alphabetical order.
- Look for ☾ to find recommended sights, restaurants, nightlife, shops, arts and leisure, and hotels.

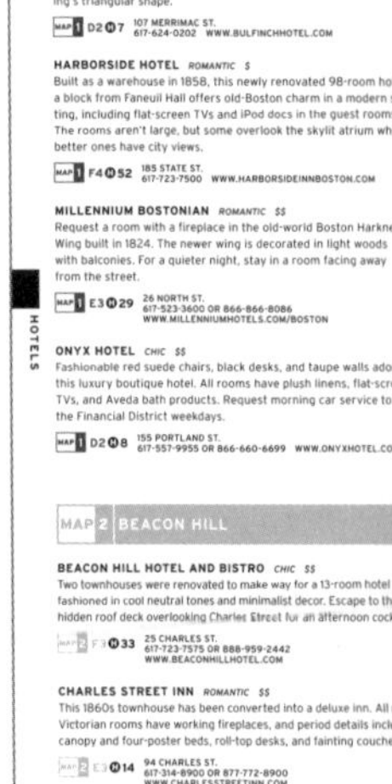

MAP 1 NORTH END/GOVERNMENT CENTER

BULFINCH HOTEL *CHIC $$*
This nine-story former industrial building has been transformed into a sleek boutique hotel with minimalist furnishings and high-speed Internet. The 80 guest rooms vary in size due to the building's triangular shape.

MAP 1 D2 H 7 107 MERRIMAC ST. 617-624-0202 WWW.BULFINCHHOTEL.COM

HARBORSIDE HOTEL *ROMANTIC $*
Built as a warehouse in 1858, this newly renovated 98-room hote a block from Faneuil Hall offers old-Boston charm in a modern se ting, including flat-screen TVs and iPod docs in the guest rooms. The rooms aren't large, but some overlook the skylit atrium while better ones have city views.

MAP 1 F4 H 52 185 STATE ST. 617-723-7500 WWW.HARBORSIDEINNBOSTON.COM

MILLENNIUM BOSTONIAN *ROMANTIC $$*
Request a room with a fireplace in the old-world Boston Harkness Wing built in 1824. The newer wing is decorated in light woods with balconies. For a quieter night, stay in a room facing away from the street.

MAP 1 E3 H 29 26 NORTH ST. 617-523-3600 OR 866-866-8086 WWW.MILLENNIUMHOTELS.COM/BOSTON

HOTELS

ONYX HOTEL *CHIC $$*
Fashionable red suede chairs, black desks, and taupe walls adorn this luxury boutique hotel. All rooms have plush linens, flat-scree TVs, and Aveda bath products. Request morning car service to the Financial District weekdays.

MAP 1 D2 H 8 155 PORTLAND ST. 617-557-9955 OR 866-660-6699 WWW.ONYXHOTEL.COM

MAP 2 BEACON HILL

BEACON HILL HOTEL AND BISTRO *CHIC $$*
Two townhouses were renovated to make way for a 13-room hotel fashioned in cool neutral tones and minimalist decor. Escape to the hidden roof deck overlooking Charles Street for an afternoon cockta

MAP 2 F3 H 33 25 CHARLES ST. 617-723-7575 OR 888-959-2442 WWW.BEACONHILLHOTEL.COM

CHARLES STREET INN *ROMANTIC $$*
This 1860s townhouse has been converted into a deluxe inn. All ni Victorian rooms have working fireplaces, and period details includ canopy and four-poster beds, roll-top desks, and fainting couches.

MAP 2 E3 H 14 94 CHARLES ST. 617-314-8900 OR 877-772-8900 WWW.CHARLESSTREETINN.COM

78 MOON METRO

TWO WAYS TO NAVIGATE

1. Scan the map to see what listings are in the area you want to explore. Use the directory to find out the name and page number for each listing.

2. Read the listings to find the specific place you want to visit. Use the map information at the bottom of each listing to find the listing's exact location.

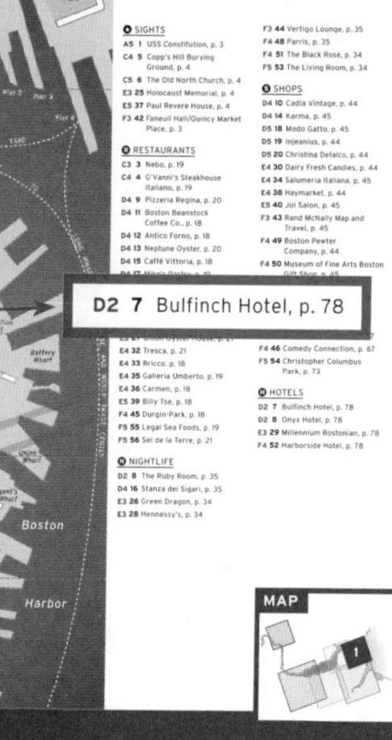

MAP KEY

Major Sights ★

MBTA Station

Shopping District

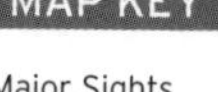

Stairs

Pedestrian Street

Adjacent Map Boundaries

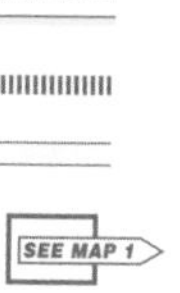

Walking Trails

SECTION ICONS

- SIGHTS
- RESTAURANTS
- NIGHTLIFE
- SHOPS
- ARTS AND LEISURE
- HOTELS

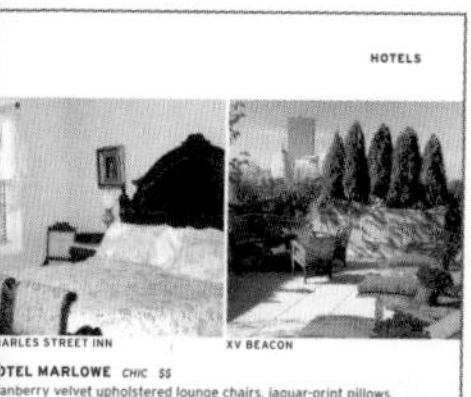

BULFINCH HOTEL *CHIC* $$

This nine-story former industrial building has been transformed into a sleek boutique hotel with minimalist furnishings and high-speed Internet. The 80 guest rooms vary in size due to the building's triangular shape.

MAP 1 D2 H 7 107 MERRIMAC ST.
617-624-0202 WWW.BULFINCHHOTEL.COM

MAP 3 DOWNTOWN/CHINATOWN

Use the **MAP NUMBER, COLOR GRID COORDINATES,** and **BLACK LOCATOR NUMBER** to find the exact location of every listing in the book.

INTRODUCTION TO BOSTON

With only 600,000 people, Boston is on the small side for a world-class city. However, it earned its stature not from the size of its population or its area, but from the size of its ideas – Boston is a city that thinks big. More than 200 years ago, Boston patriots had the big idea to brew a few million gallons of tea in the harbor and start a revolution. A hundred years ago, one Bostonian had the audacity to call the Massachusetts State House the "Hub of the Solar System" for its inordinate influence in politics and the arts. This tradition continues today, as Boston emerges from the biggest construction project ever mounted in the nation, a mammoth effort to free up public land by burying a central expressway. Its name? The Big Dig, of course.

The dust from the Dig has begun to settle, but construction was halted in 2006 after a collapse in the new tunnel killed a driver on her way to the airport. Controversy and safety concerns continue to surround the project, but the city has reclaimed an estimated 300 acres for public use, morphing the eyesore of the elevated highway into parkland, tree-lined boulevards, and restored open space. Erasing one of the skyline's ugliest elements has made room for improvements all over town – among them a convention center, a contemporary art museum, a rejuvenated waterfront, and enough cocktail lounges to outnumber its store of Irish pubs (well, almost).

In the eyes of residents, all these developments are returning Boston to its rightful place on the vanguard.

BOOKISH BOSTON

From Cambridge poet Henry Wadsworth Longfellow to noir novelist Dennis Lehane, literati have always loomed large in the local cultural landscape. A bookseller named Henry Knox was instrumental in banishing the British from Boston in 1776 – a feat he facilitated by dragging 60 tons of artillery down from Fort Ticonderoga (in upstate New York) on ox-driven sleds. The city's fame as a forum for ideas reached its peak in the 19th century, when scribes like Longfellow, Ralph Waldo Emerson, and Nathaniel Hawthorne staged their own version of the Algonquin roundtable at the Parker House hotel (now part of the Omni chain). A similar literary flowering occurred in the mid-1950s, when Robert Lowell, Sylvia Plath, and Anne Sexton were among the poets linked to the "Boston Milieu." And the city remains a formidable player on bookshelves today, claiming as residents authors including Tom Perrotta, Margot Livesey, and Robert Parker.

After all, for 100 years after the Revolution, Boston, not New York, was the de facto capital of America. Declines in the whaling and textile industries in the 19th century led the Cradle of Liberty to be gradually eclipsed by its southern rival. Boston officially dropped out of the running when the Red Sox sold Babe Ruth to the Yankees, ushering in a championship drought it took 86 years to banish.

With Bambino's Curse in the rearview and Bill Belichik in Foxborough, local sports fans have been forced to swap low expectations for the kind of smugness associated with the Yankees. The Puritan stronghold may never become a city that never sleeps, but it's shaken off Gotham's shadow in the arenas that matter most. Its picturesque downtown of winding colonial streets integrates effortlessly into a more modern metropolis, where history is as tangible as the latest trends in shopping, dining, clubbing, and entertainment.

As for Bostonians themselves, many are here for life, and they retain a proud and passionate local history – evident in the long yarns about politics, sports, and winter snowstorms that they'll share over a pint (or a trendy cocktail) downtown. All things considered, they know that a world-class city doesn't have to be the biggest, as long as it keeps having the biggest ideas.

CAPITAL OF IRISH AMERICA

Boston has been called the capital of Irish America, and certain neighborhoods are still identified with the Irish counties from which residents emigrated. But Emerald Islers haven't always had it easy in these parts – especially back in the 17th and 18th centuries, when Puritans expressed their anti-Catholic prejudice by burning effigies in an organized riot called "Pope's Day." In the first half of the 19th century, the city's complexion changed forever when waves of immigrants arrived seeking relief from the Irish Potato Famine. By 1847, the Irish constituted a full third of Boston's population, and in the ensuing century Catholicism would eclipse Protestantism as the city's most prevalent religion. Soon these citizens claimed the political power that comes with being in the majority, electing countrymen to every major office in Massachusetts and catalyzing the career of America's first Irish Catholic president, John F. Kennedy.

HISTORY

Freedom is a recurring theme in Boston's rich and eventful history, starting with the English settlers that first colonized it. Known as Puritans for their rejection of the Anglican Church and its lingering strains of Catholicism, these radical Protestants perceived the New World as a haven where they could practice their religion in peace. Before making landfall on the coast of Massachusetts, Governor John Winthrop expressed his hope that the raw space they were inhabiting would become "a city upon a hill," living proof that it's possible to build the world of one's dreams from scratch.

Winthrop's words are echoed not only in Boston's independent spirit, but also in the amiable hubris of its inhabitants. When Oliver Wendell Holmes described the State House as the "Hub of the Solar System," he was merely mouthing the beliefs of many. Such statements may seem delusional to the residents of other American cities, but Boston's belief in its own importance has allowed it to act as a catalyst in events ranging from the American Revolution to the struggle to make same-sex marriage legal.

Ideals matter: this is the message to be drawn from Paul Revere's ride, from the ardent abolitionism of

William Lloyd Garrison, from the fact that the first African American regiment to serve our country (the Massachusetts 54th, during the Civil War) was mustered in Hyde Park and dispatched from Long Wharf. Industry and immigration have changed the city's complexion from a Puritan stronghold to a polyglot melting pot, but the character of Boston remains the same. Irish Catholics may have eclipsed English Protestants in its power structure, but Boston is still a city with an elevated opinion of its own status – a conceit that has served it well in its citizens' defense of freedom and other embattled ideals.

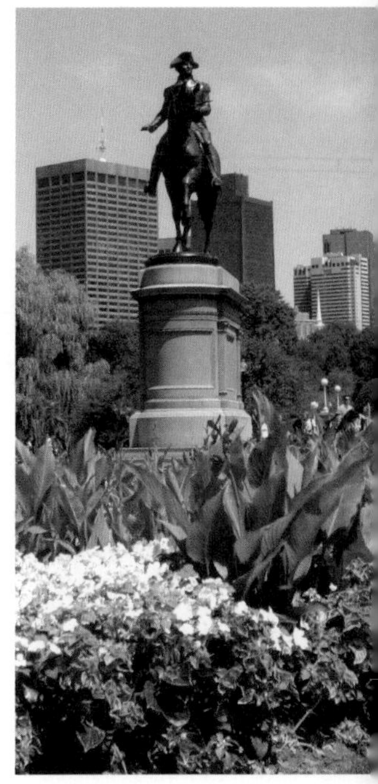

AQUATIC TAXIS

Everything you've heard about Boston drivers is true – however civilized it may seem from the sidewalk, the city shows its anger-management issues every time it gets behind the wheel. Who needs the hostility when you can escape the streets altogether in an atmospheric water taxi? Much is made of its status as a "walking city," but Boston is also a world-class water city, and aquatic options are available for just about every itinerary you might plan here. Looking to leave Logan without hitting a gridlocked tunnel? Try the **Harbor Express (p. 85),** a year-round water shuttle with direct service to destinations from Downtown to the Charlestown Navy Yard. Those seeking flexibility can hit the waves with one of two all-season taxi services (**City Water Taxi, p. 85** and **Rowes Wharf Water Taxi, p. 85**), both of which offer affordable transport to most major waterfront destinations.

THE FEDERALIST

BEACON HILL

ISABELLA STEWART GARDNER MUSEUM

BEST OF BOSTON

Any number of adventures can be had by the casual visitor to Boston who might come in search of highlights associated with history, literature, intellectual achievement, or maritime glory days. All these subplots converge in the single story of today's Boston, a sprawling epic marked by memorable characters like Paul Revere, Henry Wadsworth Longfellow, Isabella Stewart Gardner, and Ted Williams. Whole years could be spent exploring the landscape of all these legacies, but it's possible to distill a perfect itinerary from sites you can hit in a single day.

1 Fortify yourself with food fit for a Brahmin at **The Federalist (p. 22),** home of the city's best power breakfast.

2 Depending on the weather, head either to the Frog Pond ice rink on **Boston Common (p. 7)** or to the neighboring **Public Garden (p. 7)** and its iconic **Swan Boats (p. 74).**

3 From here it's an easy stroll to postcard-perfect **Beacon Hill (p. 4),** where you can imagine yourself as a Henry James protagonist while perusing the pleasing boutiques of **Charles Street (p. 46).**

4 If you only have time for one stop on the succinct **Black Heritage Trail (p. 6),** make it the **Museum of Afro-American History (p. 60),** which honors the history and contributions of African Americans in New England.

5 You haven't really been to Boston until you've bent an elbow in a local pub, and one of the city's best is the **Green Dragon (p. 34).**

6 Another Boston must-do awaits in the garlic-steeped streets of the North End, where you can find heaven on the half shell at **Neptune Oyster (p. 20).**

7 Enough rambling through revolutionary haunts – it's time to upgrade to the Gilded Age. Treat yourself to a cab and cross town to the **Isabella Stewart Gardner Museum (p. 13),** an intimate collection housed in a Venetian-style palazzo.

8 You're in the neighborhood – why not follow high art with a salute to America's pastime? On game days, **Fenway Park (p. 12)** is gridlocked, but you can still pay tribute to the Sox at the tchotchke-stocked **The Souvenir Store (p. 54)** across Yawkey Way.

9 Until recently, the Fenway cocktail scene was confined to the crowded dance clubs of Lansdowne Street. Now you can sip champagne with other swells in the brasserie-style bar at **Eastern Standard (p. 30),** a stunning new hot spot in the Hotel Commonwealth complex.

10 Time for dinner – and a cab ride back to Boston Common, which doubles as the front yard of **No. 9 Park (p. 25).** But the view isn't the only upside to this Barbara Lynch eatery, which approaches perfection in its finesse with French and Italian country cuisine.

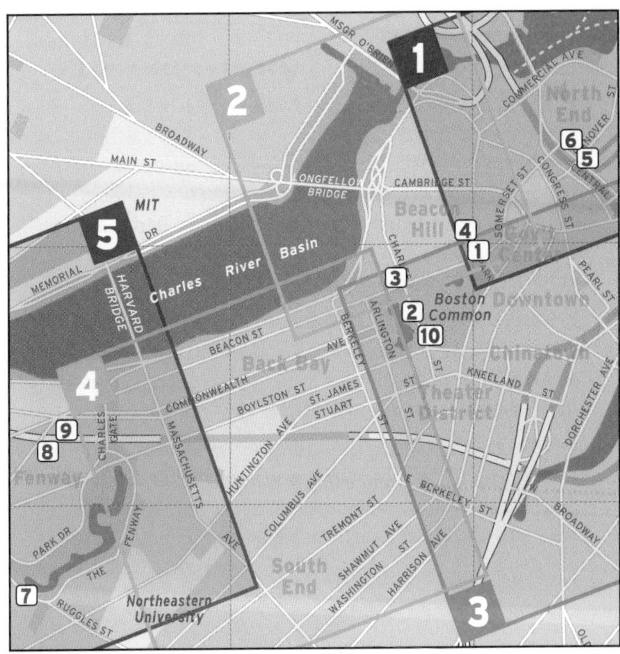

LONGFELLOW NATIONAL HISTORIC SITE

HARVEST

LOCKE-OBER

INTELLECTUAL BOSTON

You've don't need a genius IQ to make do in Boston, but the city does place a premium on ideas, innovation, and intellect. Whether you're following in the footsteps of the Transcendentalists or seeking a date who can quote Camus, you've come to a place where food for thought is never in short supply. So grab an espresso, flex your synapses, and follow our cues to the haunts (both historical and contemporary) of Boston's smart set.

1 Start the day in Cambridge with a classic New England brunch that's sure to get your intellectual juices flowing at Harvard Square's **Henrietta's Table (p. 31).**

2 You'll find the motherlode of intellectual artifacts a few blocks up Brattle Street, where Henry Wadsworth Longfellow's home is preserved as the **Longfellow National Historic Site (p. 64).** Here he entertained a who's who of 19th-century scribes, politicos, and thinkers – among them Ralph Waldo Emerson, Nathaniel Hawthorne, and Senator Charles Sumner (a noted abolitionist).

3 Head back down Brattle Street to the hub of intellectual activity, Harvard Yard, and spend a few hours exploring the mineralogical and geological galleries at the **Harvard Museum of Natural History (p. 64).**

4 After contemplating the rare gems and rocks, it's time for lunch under the trees on the outdoor patio at **Harvest (p. 31).** Here you can rub elbow patches with local scholars while nibbling on the fresh seasonal ingredients.

5 Pick up a memento of Harvard Square at the **Grolier Poetry Book Shop (p. 56),** a shrine to verse formerly frequented by T. S. Eliot, e. e. cummings, Allen Ginsberg, and others.

6 For an immersion course in left-brain breakthroughs, it's off to the **MIT Museum (p. 66),** where the exhibits include kinetic sculptures and an interactive display on robots.

7 Across the bridge in Boston, you can cover two bases by pausing for drinks at the **Last Hurrah (p. 37),** the storied bar of the **Omni Parker House (p. 80).** Named for a novel loosely based on the life of a local politico (James Michael Curley), the Last Hurrah shares a roof with Parker's Bar. Here luminaries like Emerson, Hawthorne, and John Greenleaf Whittier once gathered for a salon dubbed the Saturday Club.

8 Your intellectual quest ends at **Locke-Ober (p. 24),** where martinis once inspired Ogden Nash to verse. The menu at this landmark restaurant has found favor with a classy cast of regulars – among them President John F. Kennedy, historian Arthur M. Schlesinger, Jr., and economist John Kenneth Galbraith.

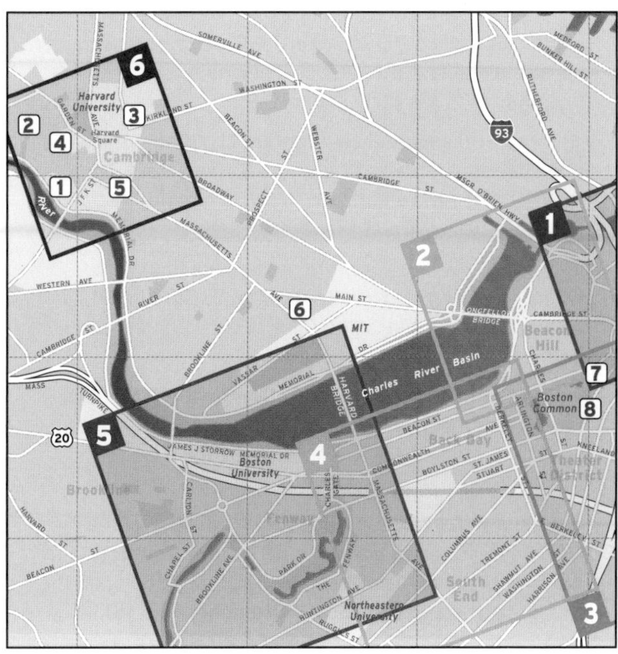

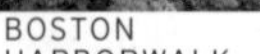
BOSTON HARBORWALK

BOSTON DUCK TOUR

USS *CONSTITUTION*

BOSTON BY SEA

It's been awhile since the harbor was crowded with clipper ships, but Boston's identity remains steeped in the sea that surrounds it. From the formerly "dirty water" of the now pristine Charles River to the miles of landscaped paths defined by the **Boston HarborWalk (p. 74),** it's easy to spend a day here without ever losing sight of the waves.

1 Grab a gourmet "lemon lust tart" from the South End's cult bakery, **Flour Bakery + Café (p. 26),** and marvel at the fact that this chic neighborhood (like the Back Bay) was formerly under water.

2 Head to the **Prudential Center (p. 10)** and practice quacking in preparation for a **Boston Duck Tour (p. 74).** When the amphibious vehicle hits the river, you may even get a turn at the wheel.

3 Head to the waterfront for some face time with fish at the fabulous **New England Aquarium (p. 9).** Afterwards take a stroll on Central Wharf and visit the harbor seals next to the ticket booth.

4 Succumb to the siren song of seafood at **The Barking Crab (p. 24),** where you can feast in front-row seats overlooking Fort Point Channel and the Financial District skyline.

5 Hop a water taxi to Charlestown and pay your respects to Old Ironsides (the **USS *Constitution* p. 3**). While here, follow **The Freedom Trail (p. 7)** through the winding streets to **Bunker Hill Monument (p. 16).**

6 Cab it to the Back Bay for a hydrating facial at **G Spa (p. 50),** then stroll up Newbury Street to **Trident Booksellers & Café (p. 53),** where you'll find copies of Dennis Lehane's Boston epic, *Mystic River.*

7 Cocktails, anyone? Hit the bar at **Top of the Hub (p. 28)** for an aerial view of the city and the rivers that run through it.

8 Before dinner, take an atmospheric turn on Long Wharf, where the clinking masts of docked boats evoke an era of maritime dominance. Then duck into **Meritage (p. 25)** for an extravagant meal with stunning views of Boston Harbor.

9 Close out the evening with a trip across the Charles to Cambridge, where big-name jazz musicians can be seen at the Charles Hotel's **Regattabar (p. 42).**

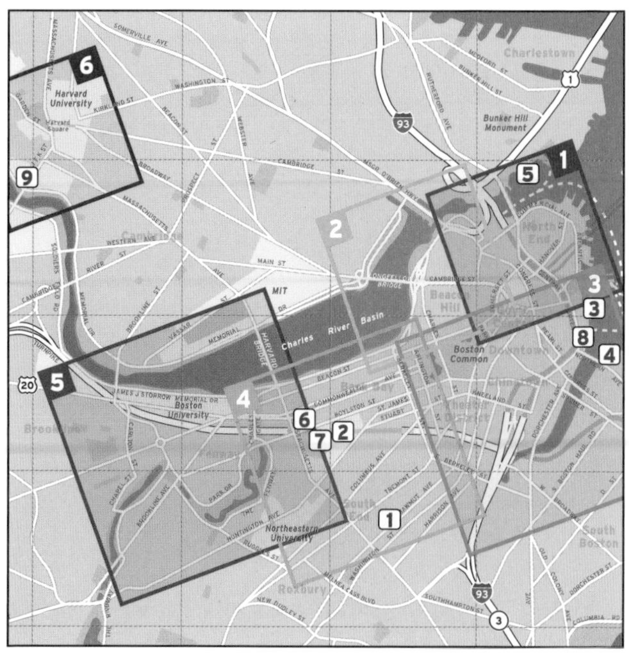

NORTH END/ GOVERNMENT CENTER

A trip to the city's North End is a journey across continents and back in time – especially in the summer, when Italian street festivals infuse narrow lanes with the ambience of Old World Europe. A walk down the main drag of Hanover Street, and it's difficult to resist the doorways of candlelit trattorias and cafés where old men linger over grappa and espresso. In other respects, the neighborhood is coolly contemporary, with upscale eateries and chic boutiques. Old North Church, where the famous lanterns were hung, is now steps from eclectic shops like Cadia Vintage, while Paul Revere's home shares its square with Carmen and Mamma Maria, evergreen favorites in Boston's dining scene.

Government Center seems bland by comparison. Anchored by the Brutalist architecture of City Hall Plaza, this is where the business of running Boston happens. The windswept swath of portland cement stands on soil formerly occupied by Scollay Square, a red-light district rife with gambling dens, tattoo parlors, and burlesque houses. Adding much-needed color is the quaint complex encompassing Faneuil Hall and Quincy Market, where historic buildings and cobblestone walkways serve as the setting for an urban walking mall.

NORTH END/ GOVERNMENT CENTER

A trip to the city's North End is a journey across continents and back in time – especially in the summer, when Italian street festivals infuse narrow lanes with the ambience of Old World Europe. A walk down the main drag of Hanover Street, and it's difficult to resist the doorways of candlelit trattorias and cafés where old men linger over grappa and espresso. In other respects, the neighborhood is coolly contemporary, with upscale eateries and chic boutiques. Old North Church, where the famous lanterns were hung, is now steps from eclectic shops like Cadia Vintage, while Paul Revere's home shares its square with Carmen and Mamma Maria, evergreen favorites in Boston's dining scene.

Government Center seems bland by comparison. Anchored by the Brutalist architecture of City Hall Plaza, this is where the business of running Boston happens. The windswept swath of portland cement stands on soil formerly occupied by Scollay Square, a red-light district rife with gambling dens, tattoo parlors, and burlesque houses. Adding much-needed color is the quaint complex encompassing Faneuil Hall and Quincy Market, where historic buildings and cobblestone walkways serve as the setting for an urban walking mall.

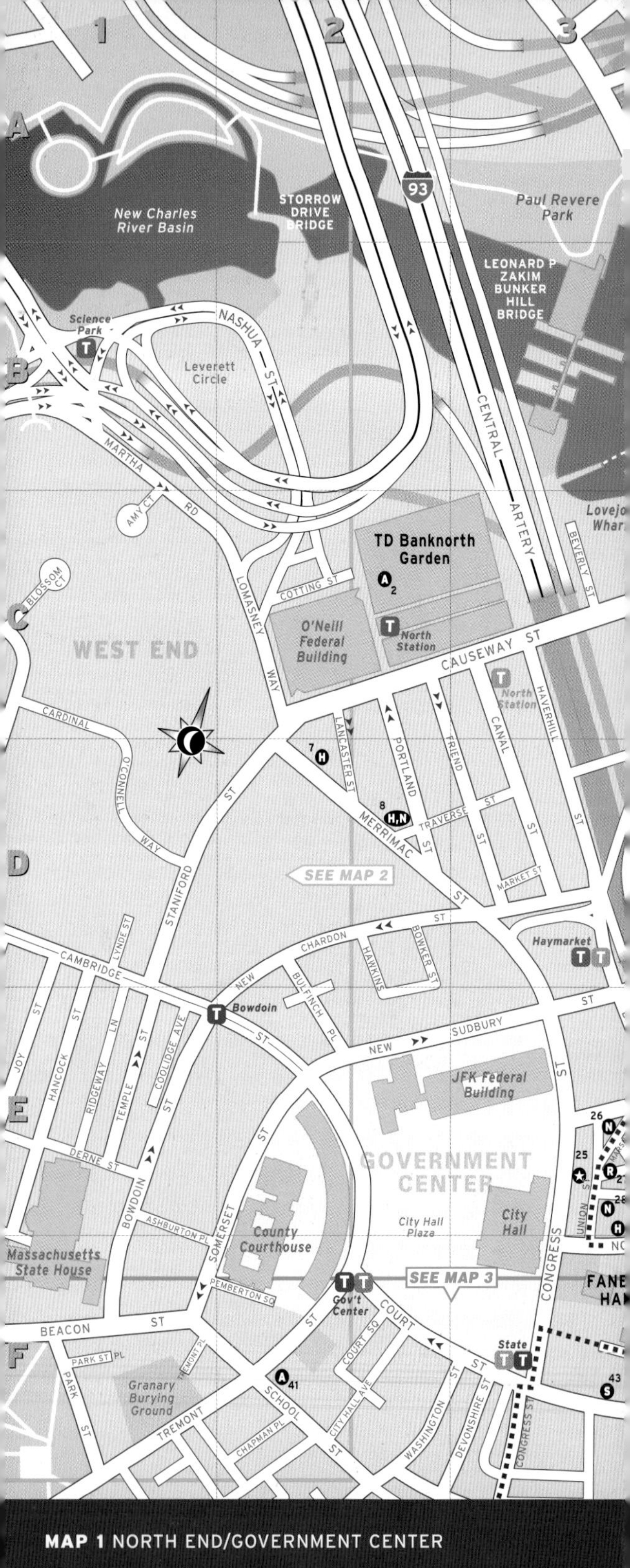

MAP 1 NORTH END/GOVERNMENT CENTER

4
5
6
USS CONSTITUTION
Hoosac Pier
Pier 1
Pier 2
CHARLESTOWN BRIDGE
FERRY TO NAVY YARD
North End Playground
NORTH END
Constitution Wharf
Union Wharf
Sargent's Wharf
Lewis Wharf
QUINCY MARKET PLACE
Christopher Columbus Park
Aquarium
Long Wharf
North Square
0.1 KM
0.1 MI
Approximate distance across map: 1 mi / 1.6 km

[6] Cab it to the Back Bay for a hydrating facial at **G Spa (p. 50),** then stroll up Newbury Street to **Trident Booksellers & Café (p. 53),** where you'll find copies of Dennis Lehane's Boston epic, *Mystic River.*

[7] Cocktails, anyone? Hit the bar at **Top of the Hub (p. 28)** for an aerial view of the city and the rivers that run through it.

[8] Before dinner, take an atmospheric turn on Long Wharf, where the clinking masts of docked boats evoke an era of maritime dominance. Then duck into **Meritage (p. 25)** for an extravagant meal with stunning views of Boston Harbor.

[9] Close out the evening with a trip across the Charles to Cambridge, where big-name jazz musicians can be seen at the Charles Hotel's **Regattabar (p. 42).**

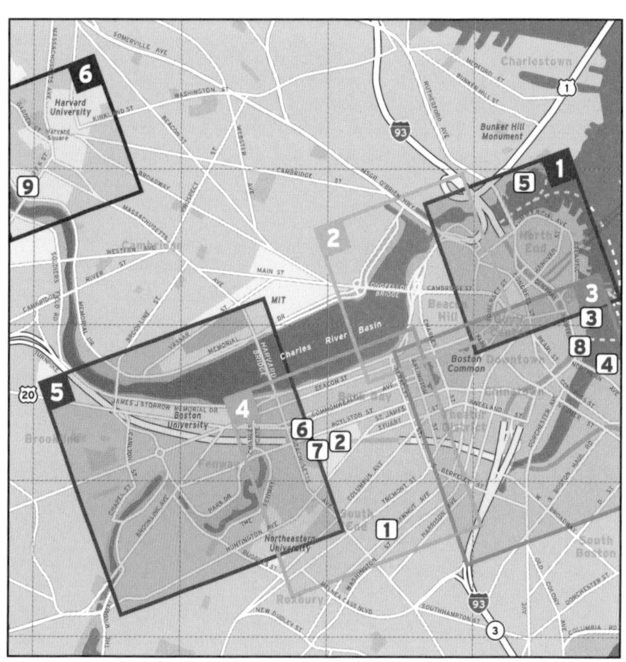

...ARF, US COURTHOUSE, AND WORLD TRADE CENTER

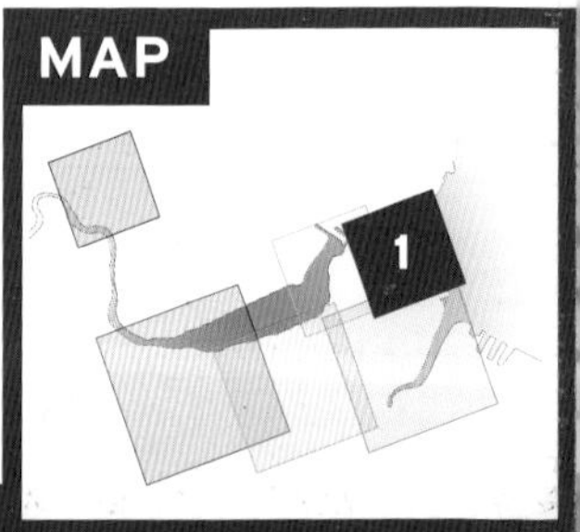

MAP 1

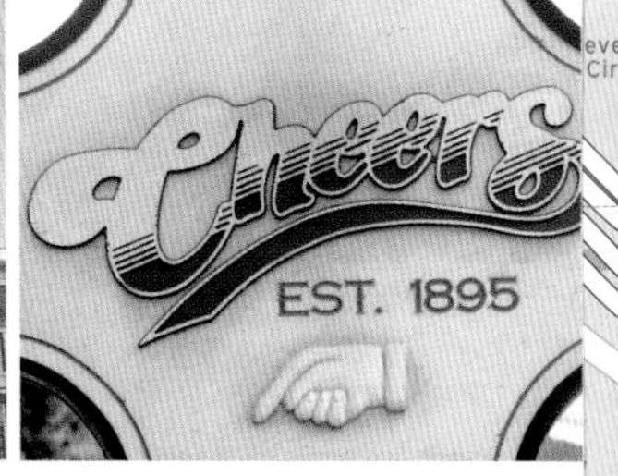

BEACON HILL

Gaslights, cobblestones, and brick buildings lend an old-world ambience to the streets of Beacon Hill, long a stronghold for Boston Brahmins, the blue-blooded New Englanders so called by Oliver Wendell Holmes. Holmes himself lived there, as have proper Bostonians from John Hancock to John Kerry. But while blue bloodlines once prevailed among owners of the Federal-style mansions and Greek Revival townhouses on the south slope, the north slope was home to the city's first African American community. The Black Heritage Trail highlights landmarks such as the African Meeting House, America's oldest standing black church and a forum for abolitionists in the 19th century.

The appeal of Beacon Hill today isn't so much in its specific attractions as in its atmosphere. At its summit stands the soaring gold dome of the Massachusetts State House, while the so-called Flat of the Hill is dominated by Charles Street, thronged with antique shops, expense-account eateries, and neo-preppie boutiques. The heart of the Hill lies in Louisburg Square, where the streets bear the ruts of coaches from the days when Louisa May Alcott was in residence.

SIGHTS

E5 **21** Black Heritage Trail, p. 6
F3 **36** ★ Beacon Hill, p. 4
F5 **39** ★ Massachusetts State House, p. 5

RESTAURANTS

A4 **3** Dante, p. 22
D4 **7** Pierrot Bistrot Française, p. 23
E3 **15** Artú, p. 21
E3 **18** Café Vanille, p. 22
E4 **19** Lala Rokh, p. 22
F3 **27** The Paramount, p. 23
F3 **29** 75 Chestnut, p. 23
F3 **30** Figs, p. 22
F3 **33** Beacon Hill Bistro, p. 21
F3 **37** The Upper Crust, p. 23
F6 **41** The Federalist, p. 22

NIGHTLIFE

D4 **6** Harvard Gardens, p. 36
E3 **17** The Sevens, p. 36
F3 **34** Cheers, p. 35
F6 **40** 21st Amendment, p. 36
F6 **43** 6B, p. 36

SHOPS

D4 **5** Savenor's Market, p. 47
E3 **11** Black Ink, p. 46
E3 **12** Charles Street, p. 46
E3 **13** Upstairs Downstairs Antiques, p. 47
E3 **16** Antiques at 80 Charles, p. 46
F3 **23** The Flat of the Hill, p. 46
F3 **24** Holiday, p. 46
F3 **25** French Dressing, p. 46
F3 **26** Moxie, p. 47
F3 **28** Wish, p. 47
F3 **31** The Beauty Mark, p. 46
F3 **32** Koo de Kir, p. 47
F3 **35** Room With a Vieux Antiques, p. 47

ARTS AND LEISURE

A4 **4** Museum of Science, p. 61
E2 **8** Community Boating, p. 73
E2 **9** Hatch Shell, p. 68
E3 **10** The Esplanade, p. 73
E5 **20** Harrison Gray Otis House, p. 60
E5 **22** Museum of Afro-American History, p. 60
F5 **38** Nichols House Museum, p. 61
F6 **44** Boston Athenaeum, p. 60

HOTELS

A3 **1** Royal Sonesta Hotel, p. 79
A3 **2** Hotel Marlowe, p. 79
E3 **14** Charles Street Inn, p. 78
F3 **33** Beacon Hill Hotel and Bistro, p. 78
F6 **42** XV Beacon, p. 79

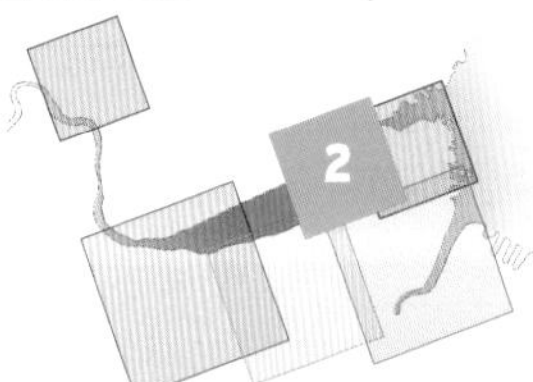

DOWNTOWN/CHINATOWN

From the aromatic alleyways of Chinatown to the concrete canyons of the Financial District, Boston's downtown is a realm easily navigated on foot. The emerald oasis of Boston Common and the Public Garden is home to iconic landmarks like Frog Pond, the Swan Boats, and, come Christmas, a towering evergreen imported from Nova Scotia. From here it's a leisurely stroll to the Theater District, an abridged version of Broadway that attracts everything from showcase musicals to artsy independent dramas. The streets become noticeably cleaner and quieter in the Financial District, where skyscrapers reach for the heavens. At their feet, the New England Aquarium is the jewel of the waterfront.

Chinatown Gate ushers you into a grotto dense with dim sum joints, sushi bars, and noodle shops. Beyond this lies the Ladder District, so named because its short parallel streets resemble rungs between the uprights formed by Tremont and Washington Streets. This noir-feeling neighborhood is the latest frontier for fashionable restaurants, lounges, and nightclubs.

SIGHTS

A2 **2** ★ Boston Common, p. 7
A3 **3** ★ The Freedom Trail, p. 7
A5 **13** Custom House, p. 10
B1 **16** ★ Public Garden, p. 7
B6 **37** ★ New England Aquarium, p. 9

RESTAURANTS

A3 **4** No. 9 Park, p. 25
B1 **18** Via Matta, p. 26
B1 **19** Aujourd'hui, p. 23
B1 **20** Finale, p. 24
B2 **22** Troquet, p. 25
B3 **25** Ivy Restaurant, p. 24
B3 **27** Locke-Ober, p. 24
B3 **34** The Good Life, p. 24
B6 **39** Meritage, p. 25
C3 **49** Chau Chow City, p. 24
C3 **51** Shabu-Zen, p. 25
C3 **52** Ginza, p. 24
C3 **53** Les Zygomates, p. 24
C4 **54** Radius, p. 25
C6 **56** The Barking Crab, p. 24

NIGHTLIFE

A3 **5** Silvertone Bar and Grill, p. 37
A3 **6** Beantown Pub, p. 36
A4 **8** Last Hurrah, p. 37
A5 **12** The Black Rhino, p. 36
B3 **26** Om Bar, p. 37
B3 **31** Felt, p. 37
C2 **47** Caprice/Underbar, p. 36
C2 **48** The Roxy, p. 37
D5 **59** Lucky's Lounge, p. 37

SHOPS

A5 **11** Ari Boston, p. 48
B1 **17** Exhale Mind/Body Spa, p. 48
B3 **28** Brattle Bookshop, p. 48
B3 **29** Filene's Basement, p. 48
B3 **33** Downtown Crossing, p. 48
B5 **36** Zareh Inc., p. 49
C2 **44** Vinh Kan Ginseng Co., p. 49
C3 **50** Vessel, p. 48

ARTS AND LEISURE

A1 **1** Swan Boats, p. 74
A4 **10** Old State House Museum, p. 62
A6 **15** Boston Harbor Islands, p. 73
B2 **21** Commonwealth Shakespeare Co., p. 68
B2 **23** Colonial Theatre, p. 68
B3 **24** Orpheum Theatre, p. 69
B3 **32** The Opera House, p. 69
B4 **35** Old South Meeting House, p. 62
C1 **40** Stuart Street Playhouse, p. 69
C2 **41** Charles Playhouse, p. 68
C2 **42** Boston Lyric Opera, p. 68
C2 **43** Wilbur Theatre, p. 69
C2 **45** Boston Ballet, p. 68
C2 **46** Wang Center for the Performing Arts, p. 69
C5 **55** Boston Tea Party Ships & Museum, p. 61
D5 **57** Boston HarborWalk, p. 74
D5 **58** Boston Children's Museum, p. 61
D6 **60** Institute of Contemporary Art, p. 62
E1 **61** Bernard Toale Gallery, p. 61

HOTELS

A4 **7** Nine Zero, p. 80
A4 **9** Omni Parker House, p. 80
A5 **14** Marriott's Custom House, p. 80
B1 **19** Four Seasons Hotel Boston, p. 79
B3 **30** Ritz-Carlton, Boston Common, p. 80
B6 **38** Boston Harbor Hotel, p. 79

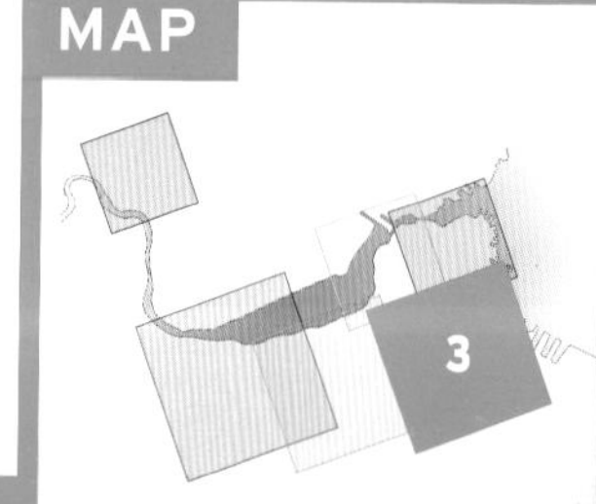

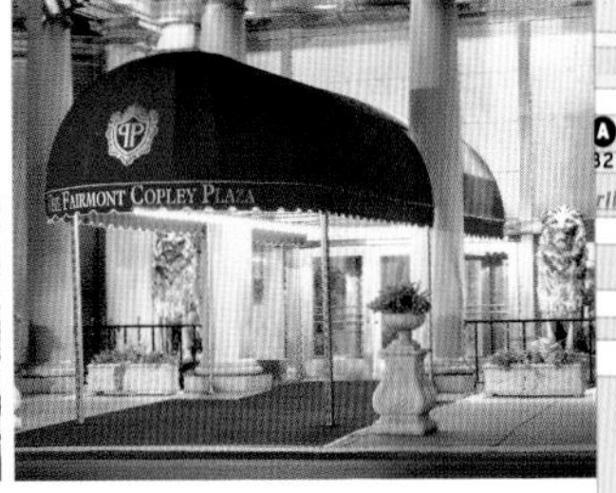

BACK BAY/SOUTH END

The Back Bay earned its name from the days when it served as an estuary of the Charles River. Little evidence of this stagnant backwater remained after Victorian visionaries imported acres of gravel to create a grid of French-style boulevards and cosmopolitan cross streets. *Mayflower* descendants may still monopolize Beacon Street's landmark brownstones, but elitism gives way to eclecticism on Newbury Street. Boston's answer to a British high street, this chic shopping row connects a suite of alphabetized cross streets, with haute options concentrated toward Arlington while Gloucester and Hereford cater to a more casual, bohemian crowd. South of Newbury is I. M. Pei's soaring John Hancock Tower, whose blue glass sides mirror older attractions like Trinity Church and Boston Public Library.

Before the Back Bay became the most desirable neighborhood in 19th-century Boston, that honor was held by the South End, which has regained its Cinderella status after a long period of decline. Now its historic row houses are home to a mix of empty nesters and hipsters, while a robust dining scene continues to evolve on Tremont Street. The Boston Center for the Arts anchors a vibrant slate of arts and theater options, and nearby South Washington Street (SoWa, to locals) is an epicenter for edgy shops, restaurants, and cocktail lounges.

SIGHTS

RESTAURANTS

NIGHTLIFE

SHOPS

ARTS AND LEISURE

HOTELS

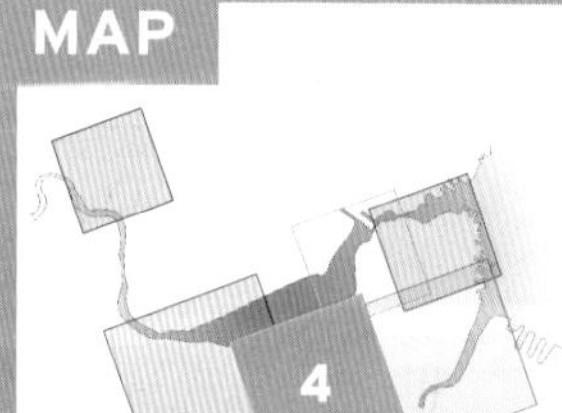

FENWAY/KENMORE SQUARE

Diamonds are a town's best friend – except when they're a haunted house, as Fenway Park became during the 86-year championship drought dubbed the Curse of the Bambino. With the Curse's storybook reversal in 2004, Red Sox Nation has let go of its trademark pessimism, and this psychological makeover is reflected in the neighborhood's resurgence. Once a place people passed through on their way to the game or Lansdowne Street's clubs, the confluence of the Fenway and Kenmore Square is now a destination in its own right – thanks largely to the Hotel Commonwealth complex, which monopolizes a city block with upscale boutiques, an underground lounge, and two world-class restaurants.

At last, the onetime stomping grounds of Isabella Stewart Gardner have evolved to suit her standards, which can be seen in the Venetian Renaissance palazzo (the Isabella Stewart Gardner Museum) that houses her extraordinary art collection. Those seeking a more comprehensive cultural experience can eye the exhibits at the nearby Museum of Fine Arts, while nature fans can forage through the Back Bay Fens – an unexpected oasis of grassy lawns, reedy ponds, stone bridges, and gardens designed by landscape architect Frederick Law Olmsted.

SIGHTS

C5 7 Citgo Sign, p. 15
D4 22 ★ Fenway Park, p. 12
F3 34 ★ Isabella Stewart Gardner Museum, p. 13
F4 37 ★ Museum of Fine Arts, p. 14

RESTAURANTS

C4 6 Game On! Sports Cafe, p. 30
C5 8 Eastern Standard, p. 30
C5 16 Great Bay, p. 30
D4 23 Sorento's, p. 31
D4 25 El Pelon Taqueria, p. 30
D6 29 Clio, p. 30
E4 30 Linwood Bar and Grill, p. 30
E4 31 Brown Sugar Café, p. 29
F3 35 The Gardner Café, p. 30

NIGHTLIFE

A1 1 The Paradise Rock Club, p. 40
C4 4 Boston Beer Works, p. 40
C4 5 Cask'n Flagon, p. 40
D3 20 Boston Billiard Club, p. 40
D4 24 Ramrod/Machine, p. 40
D5 26 Avalon, p. 39
D5 27 Axis, p. 39

SHOPS

C5 9 Commonwealth Books, p. 53
C5 10 Jean Therapy, p. 54
C5 11 Fanny and Delphine, p. 53
C5 12 Wine Gallery, p. 55
C5 13 Nantucket Natural Oils, p. 54
C5 14 Persona, p. 54
C5 15 Panopticon Gallery of Photography, p. 54
C5 17 Temper Chocolates, p. 55
C5 19 Studio for Hair, p. 55
D4 21 The Souvenir Store, p. 54

ARTS AND LEISURE

B3 2 Tsai Performance Center, p. 71
E5 32 Back Bay Fens, p. 75
E6 33 Boston Symphony Orchestra/ Symphony Hall, p. 70
F4 36 School of the Museum of Fine Arts, p. 64
F6 38 New England Conservatory, p. 71
F6 39 Huntington Theatre Co., p. 70

HOTELS

C4 3 Buckminster, p. 83
C5 18 Hotel Commonwealth, p. 83
D6 28 Eliot Hotel, p. 83

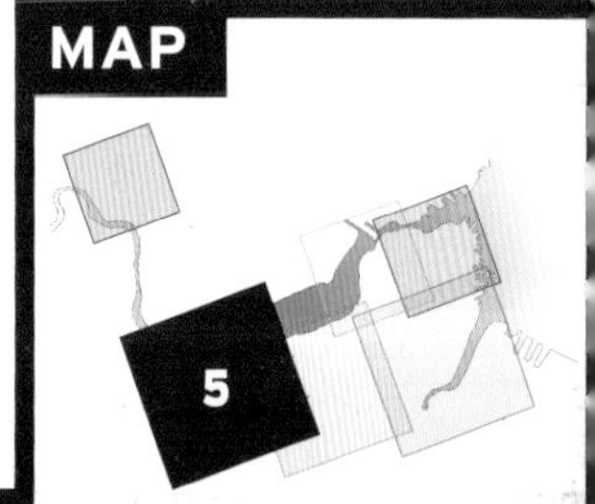

CAMBRIDGE/HARVARD SQUARE

If you spend time around Harvard Square, you'll hear locals lamenting the past decade's changes, as chain stores like Crate & Barrel and Urban Outfitters snap up leases once held by legendary diners and independent shops. Look hard enough, however, and you'll still find the "old Harvard Square," which continues to flourish in out-of-the-way enclaves like Bow and Arrow Streets (overlooked by the jester-faced facade of the Harvard Lampoon building) and Plympton Street (a Dickensian alley harboring Grolier, America's oldest continuously operating poetry bookstore).

Even an influx of brand-name franchises can't eclipse the Square's atmosphere of intellectual ferment, which owes its origins to icons like Henry Wadsworth Longfellow (whose home still stands at 105 Brattle Street) and stakes its future on today's Harvard and MIT graduates. Harvard itself is less of a square than a series of quadrangles, the most famous of which, Harvard Yard, is home to the famous John Harvard statue, whose shoe tourists are encouraged to rub for good luck. Deeper within its gates are encyclopedic holdings of art, artifacts, and ephemera, arrayed in the exhibit rooms of the Fogg, the Sackler, the Busch-Reisinger, and the Harvard Museum of Natural History.

SIGHTS

C4 9 ★ Harvard University, p. 15

RESTAURANTS

A2 1 Craigie Street Bistrot, p. 31
C2 7 Harvest, p. 31
D2 14 Rialto, p. 32
D2 15 Henrietta's Table, p. 31
D2 19 Upstairs on the Square, p. 32
D3 26 Veggie Planet, p. 32
D3 31 Om, p. 31
E3 43 Boloco, p. 31
E4 48 Mr. Bartley's Burger Cottage, p. 31

NIGHTLIFE

D2 16 Noir, p. 41
D2 17 Regattabar, p. 42
D2 20 Grendel's Den, p. 41
D3 31 Om, p. 41
E2 40 Redline, p. 42
E2 41 Shay's Pub and Wine Bar, p. 42
E4 45 Grafton Street, p. 40

SHOPS

C2 6 L. A. Burdick Chocolate, p. 56
C3 8 Museum of Useful Things, p. 57
D2 12 Comma, p. 56
D3 22 Beauty and Main, p. 55
D3 23 Mint Julep, p. 57
D3 24 The Tannery, p. 57
D3 25 Tealuxe, p. 58
D3 28 Harvard Square, p. 56
D3 29 Cardullo's, p. 55
D3 30 Curious George Goes to Wordsworth, p. 56
D3 32 Newbury Comics, p. 57
D3 33 The Harvard Coop, p. 56
D3 34 Alpha Omega, p. 55
E3 42 J. Press, p. 56
E4 46 Grolier Poetry Book Shop, p. 56
E4 47 Harvard Book Store, p. 56
E4 49 Oona's, p. 57

ARTS AND LEISURE

B1 2 Longfellow National Historic Site, p. 64
B5 4 Harvard Museum of Natural History, p. 64
C2 5 American Repertory Theatre, p. 71
C5 10 Peabody Museum of Archaeology and Ethnology, p. 65
C6 11 Semitic Museum of Harvard University, p. 65
D3 21 Brattle Theatre, p. 71
D3 27 Chess in Harvard Square, p. 75
D5 35 Sanders Theatre, p. 72
D5 36 Harvard University Art Museums, p. 64
D5 37 Harvard Film Archive, p. 72
E1 39 John F. Kennedy Park, p. 75
E3 44 Hurst Gallery, p. 64
E4 51 José Mateo's Ballet Theatre, p. 72

HOTELS

B3 3 Sheraton Commander, p. 84
D2 13 Harvard Square Hotel, p. 83
D2 18 Charles Hotel, p. 83
D6 38 Irving House, p. 84
E4 50 Inn at Harvard, p. 84

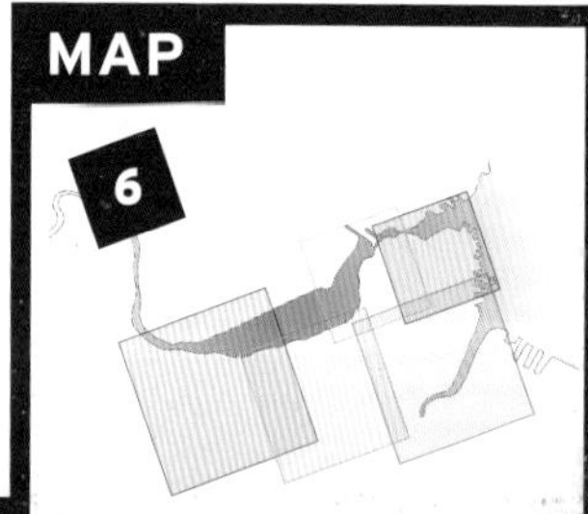

SIGHTS

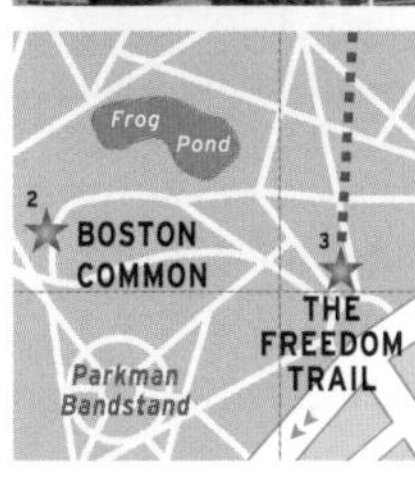

Best place to get Boston souvenirs:
FANEUIL HALL/QUINCY MARKET PLACE, p. 2

Best place to feel like a 19th-century sailor:
USS *CONSTITUTION*, p. 3

Most picturesque neighborhood for a walk: **BEACON HILL,** p. 4

Most striking rooftop: The gold dome of the
MASSACHUSETTS STATE HOUSE, p. 5

Best spring flowers: **BOSTON COMMON/PUBLIC GARDEN,** p. 7

Best walk through American history:
THE FREEDOM TRAIL, p. 7

Best giant ocean tank: **NEW ENGLAND AQUARIUM,** p. 9

Best sky-high views:
JOHN HANCOCK TOWER/PRUDENTIAL CENTER, p. 10

Most important Boston sports landmark:
FENWAY PARK's Green Monster, p. 12

Best courtyard that mixes flowers and art:
ISABELLA STEWART GARDNER MUSEUM, p. 13

Best art history lesson: **MUSEUM OF FINE ARTS,** p. 14

Best ivy-league campus: **HARVARD UNIVERSITY,** p. 15

Most chilling place to ponder what might have been:
JOHN F. KENNEDY PRESIDENTIAL LIBRARY AND MUSEUM, p. 16

FANEUIL HALL/QUINCY MARKET PLACE

Once the Cradle of Liberty, when it served as a forum for rousing Revolutionaries, Faneuil Hall (rhymes with Daniel) still attracts a boisterous crowd, but today the draw is more retail than revolutionary. Boston's wealthiest merchant, Peter Faneuil, built the hall in 1742 as a gift to the city. During the lead-up to the Revolution, many meetings among rebellious colonists took place here – they first fought the Sugar Act in the hall in 1764, establishing the creed of "no taxation without representation." The hall became the stage for some of the country's most famous orators, including Oliver Wendell Holmes and Susan B. Anthony. But retail has a long history here, as well. The lower level of Faneuil Hall was used as a market for the sale of meat, dairy, and produce.

In 1826, the granite building of Quincy Market was constructed nearby for use as wholesale food outlets. But over time the buildings became dilapidated, and Quincy Market seemed destined for the urban renewal wrecking ball. In the early 1970s, a group of Bostonians rescued the area with a major development program that restored Faneuil Hall and turned the central Quincy Market building and two adjoining buildings, North Market and South Market, into a tourist mecca that now has shops, restaurants, a comedy club, a BosTix kiosk, and outdoor sculptures.

Today the complex, with its easy access to the North End, the waterfront, and downtown, lures 20 million shoppers every year. National chains have replaced local shops, but there are a few treasures here and there, particularly at the many sales carts. Quincy Market, now filled with eateries, offers a United Nations array of treats. Faneuil Hall still remains a site for public events, including political debates. You can slip upstairs to see the famous hall or linger among the gift shops and cafés on the lower level.

FANEUIL HALL: FANEUIL HALL SQUARE
HOURS: DAILY 8 A.M.-5 P.M.
QUINCY MARKET PLACE: SOUTH MARKET BUILDING
617-523-1300
HOURS: MON.-SAT. 10 A.M.-9 P.M., SUN. NOON-6 P.M.
WWW.FANEUILHALLMARKETPLACE.COM

FANEUIL HALL

USS *CONSTITUTION*

USS *CONSTITUTION*

In 1794, the U.S. Congress authorized construction of six navy frigates to be built at Edmund Hartt's shipyard in Boston. Launched three years later, on October 21, 1797, one of these, the USS *Constitution,* went on to become one of the busiest, most successful, and, thanks to a catchy nickname, most famous battleships in U.S. history.

The *Constitution* earned its nickname during a fierce battle with HMS *Guerriere* in the War of 1812. The 18-pound cannonballs that the British fired at the ship seemed to bounce off its thick wooden sides, leading a sailor to proclaim, "Huzzah, her sides are made of iron!" From that point, the *Constitution* became Old Ironsides, a moniker that still sticks today.

The oldest commissioned warship afloat in the world, Old Ironsides was declared unseaworthy in 1830 but was restored as a result of the popular outcry caused by Oliver Wendell Holmes's emotional poem. The ship continued to sail around the world for years before finally settling down in Boston, appropriately, in 1970. Today, the 20-story-high, 300-foot-long frigate in Charlestown Navy Yard is open for tours and special events.

On land, next to the ship, the USS Constitution Museum brings its 200-plus-year history to life. Though not affiliated with the navy or the *Constitution* itself, the museum offers 3,000 original artifacts and computer-simulated reenactments and activities.

MAP 1 A5 1

CHARLESTOWN NAVY YARD 617-242-5601
SHIP TOUR HOURS: APR.-OCT. TUES.-SUN. 10 A.M.-5:50 P.M.; NOV.-MAR. THURS.-SUN. 10 A.M.-3:50 P.M. TOURS EVERY 30 MINUTES; LAST TOUR STARTS AT 3:30 P.M.
WWW.USSCONSTITUTION.NAVY.MIL
MUSEUM 617-426-1812
MUSEUM HOURS: MAY 1-OCT. 15 DAILY 9 A.M.-6 P.M.; OCT. 15-APR. 30 DAILY 10 A.M.-5 P.M.
WWW.USSCONSTITUTIONMUSEUM.ORG

COPP'S HILL BURYING GROUND

The last stop on the Boston side of the Freedom Trail, Copp's Hill is the burial site for 10,000 of the city's earliest residents. As the highest spot in the North End, it also affords terrific views.

MAP 1 C4 ✪ 5 SNOWHILL ST. AT HULL ST.

HOLOCAUST MEMORIAL

Six dramatic glass towers ascend out of the sidewalk in Carmen Park near Faneuil Hall. The numbers etched into the glass, suggesting the infamous Nazi death-camp tattoos, commemorate the six million Jews who died in the Holocaust.

MAP 1 E3 ✪ 25 CONGRESS ST., IN CARMEN PARK 617-457-8755 WWW.NEHM.ORG

THE OLD NORTH CHURCH

Made famous by the lanterns hung in the steeple to send Paul Revere on his famous ride in 1775, the church was built decades earlier in 1723 and remains an active parish to this day. Note the distinctive box pews and 1726 clock.

MAP 1 C5 ✪ 6 193 SALEM ST. 617-523-6676 WWW.OLDNORTH.COM

PAUL REVERE HOUSE

Ninety percent of this restored structure, first built in 1680 and saved by Revere's great-grandson from destruction, is original. The courtyard features a 900-pound bell made by Paul Revere & Sons; you'll find examples of Revere's silver work throughout his house.

MAP 1 E5 ✪ 37 19 NORTH SQUARE 617-523-2338 WWW.PAULREVEREHOUSE.ORG

MAP 2 BEACON HILL

BEACON HILL

The last of the three "mountains" that once stood at the center of the city, Beacon Hill is the postcard picture of Boston. Its gas lamps and cobblestone streets give a 19th-century feel to this area that has been the home to many famous past, present, and fictional Bostonians. John Hancock, Louisa May Alcott, Nathaniel Hawthorne, and Robert Frost are among the historical figures who once resided on the hill. Television's Ally McBeal also lived here, and today it's the real-life setting for some of Boston's wealthiest citizens.

In addition to their occupants, the brownstone buildings themselves, most of them more than 200 years old, give the hill much of its character. These Greek Revival-style buildings are largely the work of noted 19th-century archi-

SIDE WALKS

After a morning tour of the gold standard of government buildings, the Massachusetts State House, brunch among Brahmins at the **Beacon Hill Bistro (p. 21),** a charming restaurant that many Hill residents regard as a home away from their brownstones.

Then head for **The Esplanade (p. 73)** and take a leisurely walk along the banks of the Charles or plan to take a ride down the river in an authentic Venetian gondola shipped from Italy.

Saunter over to **Charles Street (p. 46)** and peruse the elegant antiques shops, high-end boutiques, and European-style grocers.

Make a left down Beacon Street and visit the **Boston Athenaeum (p. 60),** one of the oldest and most illustrious independent libraries in America.

tect Charles Bulfinch, or a copy of his thinking. Bulfinch himself lived on the hill and designed many of his friends' homes, most notably the three-story redbrick house at the corner of Cambridge and Lynde Streets for one-time Boston mayor Harrison Gray Otis. Today the house is open for public viewing, giving you a chance to get a taste of old-time Brahmin life. The home is full of surprises, including false doors and outlandish color schemes. Embodying the feel of the neighborhood is Louisburg Square, where Louisa May Alcott once lived and where former presidential contender and Senator John Kerry still lives.

But a visit to Beacon Hill gives a glimpse of the "other" Boston. The area was once home to a vibrant free black population – many former slaves – who made the area a hotbed of abolition sentiment. The Black Heritage Trail begins here on Joy Street near the African Meeting House. At 18 Philips Street is the marvelous Vilna Shul (www.bcjh.org), a historic synagogue now under restoration as a showcase for chronicling Jewish life in Boston.

End your trip with a stroll down Charles Street, Beacon Hill's main commercial drag – pick up an antique or spend an intimate evening in one of the many romantic restaurants.

36 BTWN. BEACON AND CAMBRIDGE STS., BOWDOIN AND CHARLES STS.

MASSACHUSETTS STATE HOUSE

Only in Boston can a building that dates back to 1798 be considered the new State House, but the Charles Bulfinch-designed, gold-topped edifice across from Boston Common is just that. Today, it houses the daily workings of the Commonwealth of Massachusetts and,

MASSACHUSETTS STATE HOUSE

BOSTON COMMON/PUBLIC GARDEN

in the often quoted and misquoted words of Oliver Wendell Holmes, stands as the "Hub of the Solar System" – usually inflated to "Universe." The oldest building on Beacon Hill, the State House boasts a connection with some prominent figures in the early history of the United States. The land on which it sits was once John Hancock's meadow, and then-Governor Samuel Adams and Paul Revere put the structure's keystone in place in 1795. The house's landmark dome underwent iterations of wood and copper before it glowed with a layer of 23-karat gold. (During the blackouts of World War II, however, the roof received a coat of black paint in order to camouflage the building.)

Inside the State House, the layout is a series of rectangular rooms, the largest being the House of Representatives chambers. Statues on the State House grounds include that of Mary Dyer, a martyred Quaker woman who refused to alter her religious beliefs and was hanged on the Common, and John F. Kennedy. An art collection just outside Doric Hall honors all Massachusetts women who were active in public life. State House tours, both guided and self-guided, are free and available daily.

MAP 2 F5 ✪39 BEACON ST. AT PARK ST. 617-727-3676
HOURS: MON.-FRI. 10 A.M.-4 P.M.
WWW.SEC.STATE.MA.US/TRS/TRSIDX.HTM

BLACK HERITAGE TRAIL

This 1.6-mile walk highlights the 19th-century antislavery movement and the strong African American community that lived here in the 1800s. Sites include several Underground Railroad stops and the Robert Gould Shaw and 54th Regiment Memorial, the famed August Saint-Gaudens sculpture of the black Civil War regiment celebrated in the movie *Glory*.

E5 ✪21 PICK UP MAP AT THE MUSEUM OF AFRO-AMERICAN HISTORY, 46 JOY ST.
617-725-0022 WWW.AFROAMMUSEUM.ORG/TRAIL.HTM

MAP 3 DOWNTOWN/CHINATOWN

BOSTON COMMON/PUBLIC GARDEN

The oldest public park in the United States was created in 1640 when 50 acres of Boston were set aside as public land. Along with the adjacent 25-acre Public Garden, these open spaces are a playground for residents and visitors alike, especially when the snow melts and spring blossoms.

At any time of year, the Common is a recreational haven for the city. The Common has also seen success as an outdoor stage. The Boston Lyric Opera's first free showing of *Carmen* on the Common drew more than 50,000 people – who came bearing blankets and picnic baskets – on consecutive nights. Shakespeare on the Common during the summer is an annual crowd-pleaser.

Across Charles Street, the more colorful and shaded Public Garden, the oldest botanical garden in the country, doesn't have the open space of the Common, but it offers more whimsy. The shallow lagoon is always filled in the summer with white fiberglass swan boats paddling by the weeping willow trees and under footbridges. The famous set-in-Boston children's tale, *Make Way for Ducklings* by Robert McCloskey, is celebrated with Nancy Schon's sculptures of eight bronze ducklings trailing their mallard mother, who is the perfect size for toddlers to climb upon. Other art here includes a famous statue of General George Washington atop his horse.

MAP 3 A2 2 BOSTON COMMON: BTWN. CHARLES AND TREMONT STS., BEACON AND BOYLSTON STS.

MAP 3 B1 16 PUBLIC GARDEN: BTWN. ARLINGTON AND CHARLES STS., BEACON AND BOYLSTON STS.
WWW.CITYOFBOSTON.GOV/PARKS

THE FREEDOM TRAIL

Connecting 18 historic landmarks with a simple red line on the sidewalk, the Freedom Trail tells the story of the Revolution and the country's path toward liberty.

The idea for the trail sprouted in 1951 when local journalist William Schofield set out to make Boston's historic sites more accessible to residents and visitors. With Boston Common as the southern terminus and the Bunker Hill Monument at the northern end, 16 sites were chosen in between as stops on the Freedom Trail. In 1958 the red line – painted on the sidewalk in some places, embedded with bricks in others – linked the landmarks.

TRAILS AND TOURS

Boston boot heels are made for walking. Major walking tours include **The Freedom Trail (p. 7),** the **Black Heritage Trail (p. 6),** and the **Boston HarborWalk (p. 74).** The premiere outlet for Beantown walking tours is **Boston By Foot** (617-367-3766 and 617-367-2345, www.bostonbyfoot.com), where knowledgeable volunteers lead tours on a variety of topics, including literary landmarks and great engineering feats, or by neighborhood, including the North End, Chinatown, and Beacon Hill. The **Boston Women's Heritage Trail** (www.bwht.org) highlights contributions of Boston women, and **Boston Movie Tours** (866-668-4345, www.bostonmovietours.net) invites you to experience Boston as depicted by Hollywood.

If your feet give out, opt to see Boston by bus, trolley, or duck on the **Boston Duck Tours (p. 74). Old Town Trolley Tours** (617-269-7150, www.oldtowntrolley.com) offers general tours of Boston plus a special **Ghosts & Gravestones Tour** (617-269-3626, www.ghostsandgravestones.com). The more scientifically inclined can take the **Innovation Odyssey** (617-350-0358, www.bostoninnovation.org), offered monthly by the Boston History Collaborative, in which live actors reenact Boston breakthroughs, including the invention of the telephone.

Starting at the Common, the stops are the State House, Black Heritage Trail, Park Street Church, Granary Burying Ground, King's Chapel, King's Chapel Burying Ground, Benjamin Franklin's Statue/site of the first public school, Old Corner Bookstore Building, Old South Meeting House, Old State House, site of the Boston Massacre, Faneuil Hall, Paul Revere House, Old North Church, Copp's Hill Burying Ground, and USS *Constitution*. At the Granary Burying Ground, which is guarded by a huge Egyptian-style gate, you'll find the graves of some of the most famous patriots, including Samuel Adams, Paul Revere, and John Hancock. The 1713 Old State House (as opposed to the 1798 new State House) is Boston's oldest public building, and right out front is the Boston Massacre site. The second-to-last stop on the Boston side of the harbor is one of the city's most recognizable landmarks, the "one if by land, two if by sea" Old North Church.

NEW ENGLAND AQUARIUM

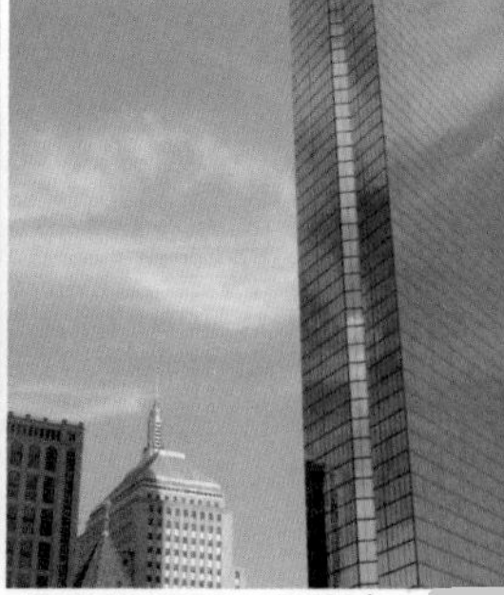

JOHN HANCOCK TOWER/ PRUDENTIAL CENTER

Altogether, the Freedom Trail is a pleasant 2.5-mile walk through downtown, Beacon Hill, the North End, and into Charlestown. There are two ways to see the trail: the do-it-yourself method or with a guided tour given by the volunteer, nonprofit foundation that maintains the trail. Many of the individual stops also offer guided tours.

START AT THE GREATER BOSTON CONVENTION & VISITORS CENTER, 147 TREMONT ST. 888-733-2678, 617-357-8300
WWW.THEFREEDOMTRAIL.ORG
VISITOR CENTER HOURS: MON.-SAT. 8:30 A.M.-5 P.M., SUN. 9 A.M.-5 P.M.

NEW ENGLAND AQUARIUM

More than a spot to gawk at pretty fish, the New England Aquarium celebrates all things aquatic from sea to shoreline. Even before stepping through the door, get close and personal with playful harbor seals in the glassed-in tank on the outside plaza. Inside, the aquarium's central feature is a 24-foot-deep, 200,000-gallon tank that replicates a Caribbean coral reef, awash with more than 120 species, including nurse sharks, sand tiger sharks, barracudas, and a venerable turtle dubbed Myrtle. Other exhibits showcase ethereal jellyfish, bizarre sea dragons, electric eels, and voracious piranhas. With three species of penguins and a seal exhibit, furred and feathered folk also get their due.

But the aquarium is not just about marveling at the sea's strange and exotic inhabitants; the institution is dedicated to conservation and whale- and dolphin-rescue efforts. Visitors can look into a functioning lab to watch researchers and biologists at work. At the "Edge of the Sea" exhibit, visitors can touch and closely examine creatures that live along the New England shore, such as starfish, horseshoe crabs, and periwinkles.

Other exhibits showcase efforts to save and protect the earth's oceans.

CENTRAL WHARF OFF ATLANTIC AVE. 617-973-5200
HOURS: MON.-FRI. 9 A.M.-6 P.M., SAT.-SUN., 9 A.M.-7 P.M.;
IMAX, DAILY 9:30 A.M.-10:30 P.M.
WWW.NEAQ.ORG

CUSTOM HOUSE

When a 495-foot tower was added in 1915 to the city's 1847 Custom House, the building became Boston's first skyscraper. Note the details on the clock and take a tour to the observation deck on the 26th floor for a 360-degree view of the city. It's now part of the Marriott Hotel.

3 MCKINLEY SQUARE
617-310-6300

JOHN HANCOCK TOWER/PRUDENTIAL CENTER

At 759 feet, the 52-floor Prudential Center tower was Boston's tallest building from 1965 until 1976, when the 62-story, 790-foot John Hancock Tower went up just three blocks away. Today both buildings would just be two more skyscrapers in cities like New York or Chicago, but in Boston they define the horizon. The flashing blue or red colors of the radio tower atop the Prudential, for example, will signal clear skies, clouds, rain, snow, or a canceled Red Sox game. Staring up at John Hancock while lying on the grass of Copley Square is an experience in itself. A photographer's dream, the angular, blue-mirrored tower designed by I. M. Pei produces picture-perfect reflections of two of Boston's oldest churches in its glass sides. And the 10,344 panes themselves became an urban legend. Thanks to an unexpected wind tunnel created inside the building, the windows developed a peculiar and dangerous habit of popping out of their frames and crashing onto the sidewalk. The problem has since been corrected.

The Hancock's observatory has been closed since September 11, 2001, but you can get a view of the city from more staid Prudential Center, which offers a 360-degree view of the Harbor Islands and Cambridge from its glitzy 52nd-floor restaurant, Top of the Hub, and its 50th-floor Skywalk Observatory. On a clear day, you can see the Cape Cod beaches to the south and New Hampshire's White Mountains to the north. An admission ticket

THE CHANGING SKYLINE

Visitors to Boston might think the entire city is under construction, and they're almost right; most of the new construction, however, has been *under* Boston, as the state relocates I-93 beneath the city.

The Central Artery/Tunnel Project – popularly called the **Big Dig** – has led to the building of such landmarks as the striking **Leonard P. Zakim Bunker Hill Bridge** (www.leonardpzakimbunkerhillbridge.org), the world's widest cable-stayed bridge, connecting Boston with Cambridge and parts north. The odd name was a political compromise between supporters of Lennie Zakim, a popular human-rights activist, and the Charlestown community, which wanted to highlight the **Bunker Hill Monument** **(p. 16).** (Towers on the bridge echo the monument's distinct shape.)

Indeed, while Bostonians love to hate the over-budget, oft-delayed, and scandal-plagued Big Dig, they like naming its components after beloved figures. The **Ted Williams Tunnel,** which goes under Boston Harbor to Logan Airport, celebrates the baseball player, and the **Thomas P. "Tip" O'Neill Tunnel** (which connects north and south highways) salutes the canny politician.

The multibillion-dollar project, intended to smooth traffic flow, is drawing to a close. Eventually the construction zones will be turned into green space. In the meantime, check www.masspike.com/bigdig/index.html for updates. Visitors should be aware that traffic patterns often change and head-pounding snarls – particularly at rush hour – should be anticipated.

includes an audio tour, a film, and access to "Dreams of Freedom," an exhibit on immigration. The shopping center on the Pru's lower levels features some of the city's most exclusive (and expensive) shops.

MAP 4 C5 ✪52 JOHN HANCOCK TOWER: 200 CLARENDON ST. 617-572-6000

MAP 4 C3 ✪39 PRUDENTIAL CENTER: 800 BOYLSTON ST. 617-236-3100 SHOP HOURS: MON.-SAT. 10 A.M.-9 P.M., SUN. 11 A.M.-6 P.M. SKYWALK OBSERVATORY HOURS: NOV.-FEB DAILY 10 A.M.-8 P.M.; MAR.-OCT. 10 A.M.-9:30 P.M. WWW.PRUDENTIALCENTER.COM

THE FIRST CHURCH OF CHRIST, SCIENTIST

World headquarters of the Christian Science movement, the 1894 Mother Church is complemented by a long reflecting pool. Nearby is the Mary Baker Eddy Library, housed in a 1934 building, with its celebrated Mapparium, a 30-foot stained-glass globe you can walk into and experience the world as it was configured in 1935. The library has changing exhibits and houses the *Christian Science Monitor;* you can see the newsroom from a glassed-in gallery.

MAP 4 D2 60 MOTHER CHURCH: 175 HUNTINGTON AVE.
617-450-2000 WWW.TFCCS.COM, 617-450-7000 OR 888-222-3711 WWW.MARYBAKERLIBRARY.ORG

TRINITY CHURCH

This church's reflection in the Hancock Tower's blue-mirrored windows from St. James Street is one of the most photographed images in all of Boston. Inside, find La Farge murals and brilliant stained-glass windows and an unusual shop with exclusive jewelry and gifts.

MAP 4 C5 50 206 CLARENDON ST. ENTER FROM COPLEY SQUARE
617-536-0944 WWW.TRINITYCHURCHBOSTON.ORG

MAP 5 FENWAY/KENMORE SQUARE

FENWAY PARK

The yearly heartbreak of the long-suffering "Fenway Faithful" finally ended in October 2004 when the Boston Red Sox won the World Series for the first time since 1918. That glorious victory has not dimmed fans' love of their team, nor their affection for their cozy breadbox of a ballpark – the oldest (opened in 1912) and just about the smallest (capacity roughly 38,000) in the Major League. Boston will always be a baseball town, never mind that the New England Patriots are regular Super Bowl champs. The city has even named a major artery – the Ted William Tunnel – after a beloved slugger.

Game day in Boston begins hours before the first pitch. Fans stream in from all directions, most of them coming up from the Kenmore Square T station. The aromas of roasted nuts, sausages, cotton candy, and beer waft through the air. Inside the park, you'll see the famous 37-foot-high left-field wall known as the Green Monster, now topped with the addition of coveted seats. Expect fans to be raucous and passionate; the decibel level will double if the Red Sox are playing their fierce rivals, the New York Yankees. Indeed, most fans consider the team's come-back-from-the-dead 2004 American League Championship (down three games against the Yankees, the Sox won the next four) just as significant a victory as the World Series itself. After all, many blamed

TRINITY CHURCH

FENWAY PARK

the 86-year dry spell on the Curse of the Bambino, reputedly made when Babe Ruth was traded from the Red Sox to the Yankees. So think twice about wearing that Yankees cap on game day and instead, gobble a Fenway Frank and root along with the folks who have stuck with the hometown team through both good times and bad.

MAP 5 D4 22 4 YAWKEY WAY 617-267-9440 WWW.REDSOX.COM

ISABELLA STEWART GARDNER MUSEUM

The Isabella Stewart Gardner Museum pays tribute to the unique artistic vision of Isabella Stewart Gardner, a wealthy Boston doyenne who loved both art and defying convention. The museum – where she also once lived – is packed with 2,500 pieces of artwork, all chosen and carefully positioned by her. The museum also carries on musical and floral traditions she established, including a Sunday concert series and an artist-in-residence program. However, the museum remains most notorious for the dramatic 1990 theft of 13 masterworks, including pieces by Vermeer, Rembrandt, and Degas – one of the largest art heists in history. Since Mrs. Gardner's will specified her museum must remain exactly as she designed it, cards mark the location of the purloined works.

Walking through the three floors of galleries can be a bit discombobulating, as Mrs. Gardner's collecting habits were as eclectic as her style. Unusual touches abound: An antique bed set finds new life as a stairway railing, and fabric from an old gown is used as a wall covering. The permanent collection includes impressive tapestries, and paintings by Botticelli, Rembrandt, Titian, Degas, Whistler, and Matisse. Mrs. Gardner also championed John Singer Sargent, who painted a then-scandalous portrait of her. She also built a gallery in the style of a Spanish cloister just to house his large masterpiece *El Jaleo*. The café often features menus tied to the museum, including nasturtium dishes in April. The Gardner is planning an expansion to increase space for changing exhibits and other events, although at this point there are no plans for closing parts of the museum to the public.

280 THE FENWAY 617-566-1401
HOURS: TUES.-SUN. 11 A.M.-5 P.M. ENTRANCE CLOSES AT 4:20 P.M.
WWW.GARDNERMUSEUM.ORG

MUSEUM OF FINE ARTS

Boston's oldest museum, the Museum of Fine Arts (MFA) has become a must-see spot for art lovers, not only for the stunning breadth of its holdings but for its collection of iconic American and European art. The Impressionists are well represented; the MFA has one of the largest groups of paintings by Claude Monet outside France. Complement a Freedom Trail jaunt by perusing the museum's displays of Americana, in particular the stunning silver work by Paul Revere (a better artist than horseman, truth be told). Explore ancient culture in the Egyptian art and mummies galleries. Visit the Far East via the extensive Chinese and Japanese art collection and the museum's peaceful outdoor Zen garden.

But MFA director Malcolm Rogers also pushes the envelope of the question "What is art?" with controversial and popular exhibits and installations on themes such as automobiles.

Founded in 1870, the MFA moved to its neoclassical building on Huntington Avenue in 1909; a major expansion is planned to provide a larger space for its American Art and add a glass-enclosed garden court. The museum will stay open throughout the expansion, and while a few galleries and spaces might be closed, the disruption will be minimal. With First Fridays (held the first Friday of the month and every Friday in summer), the museum has one of the city's hottest and most age-diverse singles scenes, with live music and cocktails. Also popular is its film series. After an afternoon of high art, take a break in one of the three restaurants.

465 HUNTINGTON AVE. 617-267-9300
HOURS: WED.-FRI. 10 A.M.-9:45 P.M., SAT.-TUES. 10 A.M.-4:45 P.M.
WWW.MFA.ORG

CITGO SIGN

This 60-foot neon Citgo sign in Kenmore Square is iconic to the Fenway, and when you see its flashing red-and-white glow, you know that Red Sox fans aren't far away.

C5 7 COMMONWEALTH AVE. AT KENMORE SQUARE T-STOP

MAP 6 CAMBRIDGE/HARVARD SQUARE

HARVARD UNIVERSITY

With a history and reputation that spans more than three and a half centuries, Harvard, or "Hahvid" as it sounds off a local's tongue, is the oldest university in the United States.

Founded in 1636, Harvard is quintessential Ivy League – redbrick buildings drizzled with the climbing green vine are what you'll see all over campus. While exploring the grounds on a guided tour or with a leisurely stroll, you'll encounter a number of landmarks. The statue of John Harvard, known as the "Statue of Three Lies" (the inscription states three facts, "John Harvard, Founder, 1638," and each is a falsehood), sits in front of University Hall, on the east side of the central yard. Located across the Old Yard, the 1720 Massachusetts Hall is the oldest building on the Harvard campus and the second oldest academic building in the country. Wandering farther north and east, be sure to stop inside the beautiful Sanders Theatre to see the unique 180-degree design that gives it such amazing acoustics.

MAP 6 C4 9

HARVARD UNIVERSITY EVENTS AND INFORMATION CENTER:
1350 MASSACHUSETTS AVE.
617-495-1573
HOURS: MON-SAT. 9 A.M.-5 P.M.
WWW.HARVARD.EDU

SIDE WALKS

After strolling the ivy-covered campus of Harvard, head across the street to the **Hurst Gallery (p. 64)** and check out the impressive collection of African, Asian, and Oceanic art.

In the same block, make your way over to **Upstairs on the Square (p. 32)** for a sprightly lunch in the fuchsia-and-violet-hued dining room. Linger for a while and enjoy a traditional afternoon tea.

Walk off your meal along Brattle Street. Stroll past the historic manors of Cambridge's Brahmin clan and browse the unique shops and boutiques, stopping in **Museum of Useful Things (p. 57)** for usual home accessories and gifts.

After shopping, plan to catch what is sure to be an engaging stage production at the **American Repertory Theatre (p. 71).**

OVERVIEW AND OFF MAP

JOHN F. KENNEDY PRESIDENTIAL LIBRARY AND MUSEUM

In an eerie, darkened hallway, a CBS commentator breaks the news to the world that the nation's 35th president has been assassinated. At the John F. Kennedy Library and Museum, this installation is among the millions of artifacts that try to capture JFK's life – and death – in vivid and minute detail.

Kennedy's legacy is alive and well around Boston – landmarks named after him and plaques of his most famous quotes can be found all over the city. But only this 18,000-square-foot museum and adjoining 135,000-square-foot library put Massachusetts's favorite son into context and remind us of his passion for public service.

The numbers tell how authoritative the collection is: 8.4 million pages of Kennedy's personal, congressional, and presidential papers; 34 million pages of manuscripts; 400,000 photographs; 9,000 hours of audio recordings; 7.5 million feet of film; and hundreds of letters, cartoons, magazines, and even college transcripts. All serve to show just how much this dashing young politician and his wife and children captivated a country.

Designed by I. M. Pei and dedicated in 1979 by President Jimmy Carter, this dramatic concrete tower sits on a 10-acre park overlooking the water. Inside the museum, visitors are immediately greeted with a gallery of touching photos and a 17-minute film that traces Kennedy's life up to his 1960 presidential nomination.

Located on Columbia Point, approximately four miles south of downtown, the museum is a little out of the way, but visitors can access it by public transportation. Free shuttle buses to the site, which run 8 A.M.-5 P.M., leave every 20 minutes from the JFK/UMASS station on the Red Line.

OFF MAP
COLUMBIA POINT 617-514-1600 OR 866-JFK-1960
HOURS: DAILY 9 A.M.-5 P.M.
WWW.JFKLIBRARY.ORG

BUNKER HILL MONUMENT

A memorial to the famous battle, the Bunker Hill obelisk is the city's greatest reminder of the Revolutionary War. A harbor view awaits at the top of the 294 steps inside.

OVERVIEW MAP **B5**
CHARLESTOWN, MONUMENT SQUARE
617-242-5641
WWW.NPS.GOV/BOST/BUNKER_HILL.HTM

RESTAURANTS

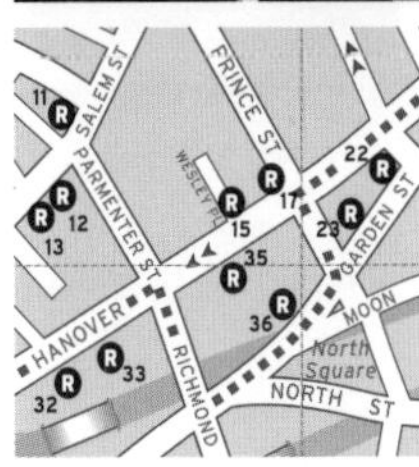

Hottest restaurant of the moment: **STELLA,** p. 28

Most romantic: **TOP OF THE HUB,** p. 28

Best weekend brunch: **STEPHANIE'S ON NEWBURY,** p. 28

Best outdoor dining: **EASTERN STANDARD,** p. 30

Best dessert: **FINALE,** p. 24

Best New England clam chowder: **LEGAL SEA FOODS,** p. 19

Best three-figure splurge: **L'ESPALIER,** p. 27

Best view with a meal: **MERITAGE,** p. 25

Best Italian pastries: **MIKE'S PASTRY,** p. 19

Best vegetarian options: **VEGGIE PLANET,** p. 32

PRICE KEY

- $ ENTRÉES UNDER $10
- $$ ENTRÉES $10–20
- $$$ ENTRÉES OVER $20

MAP 1 NORTH END/GOVERNMENT CENTER

ANTICO FORNO *QUICK BITE • ITALIAN $$*

As the name Antico Forno (Old Stove) suggests, the wood-burning oven is the focal point of this homey trattoria where you can bring the family. The Tuscan kitchen turns out pizzas, baked pastas, and hearty meats and seafood.

MAP 1 D4 R 12 93 SALEM ST. 617-723-6733 WWW.ANTICOFORNOBOSTON.COM

BILLY TSE *AFTER HOURS • ASIAN $*

Pan-Asian cooking is brought to a new level in this typically Italian neighborhood. The menu is inexpensive and offers dishes large enough to be shared among families. The sushi bar is an added bonus. Open until 11:00 P.M. weekends, 10:30 P.M. Monday-Thursday.

MAP 1 E5 R 39 240 COMMERCIAL ST. 617-227-9990 WWW.BILLYTSERESTAURANT.COM

BOSTON BEANSTOCK COFFEE CO. *BREAKFAST AND BRUNCH • ITALIAN $*

This intimate café has plushy sofas and a wood-burning fireplace for those chilly winter mornings. The coffee is high quality, and the grilled *panini* is not to be missed.

MAP 1 D4 R 11 97 SALEM ST. 617-725-0040 WWW.BOSTONBEANSTOCK.COM

BRICCO *BUSINESS • ITALIAN $$$*

This nouveau eatery offers an exceptional selection of all-Italian wines and a sophisticated five-course chef tasting. The floor-to-ceiling windows showcase the perfect place to linger over a cappuccino. Valet parking makes this a standout.

MAP 1 E4 R 33 241 HANOVER ST. 617-248-6800 WWW.BRICCO.COM

CAFFÉ VITTORIA *CAFÉ • ITALIAN $*

This was the first Italian café to open in Boston, and Italian is still the primary spoken language. Finish your evening here with a cup of espresso and a slice of ricotta pie.

MAP 1 D4 R 15 294 HANOVER ST. 617-227-7606 WWW.VITTORIACAFFE.COM

CARMEN *ROMANTIC • ITALIAN $$*

Located near Paul Revere's house, this tiny gem with tight seating offers small dishes – think Italian tapas. Snack on crostini while waiting for the wild striped bass or baked penne to arrive.

MAP 1 E4 R 36 33 NORTH SQUARE 617-742-6421

DURGIN-PARK *QUICK BITE • SEAFOOD $$*

The surly waitstaff days have passed at this touristy landmark but the tradition of serving up New England classics like Yankee pot roast continues. The family-style tables have been a staple since 1826.

MAP 1 F4 R 45 340 FANEUIL HALL MARKET PLACE 617-227-2038 WWW.DURGIN-PARK.COM

LEGAL SEA FOODS

MIKE'S PASTRY

GALLERIA UMBERTO *QUICK BITE • ITALIAN $*

The lunchtime line suggests bargain prices for pizza, calzones, *panzarotti* (potato croquettes), and *arancini* (deep-fried rice balls made with peas, cheese, and ground beef). It's only open until 2:30 P.M. so arrive early.

MAP 1 E4 R 35 289 HANOVER ST. 617-227-5709

G'VANNI'S STEAKHOUSE ITALIANO *AFTER HOURS • STEAKHOUSE $$$*

Come in for a sampling of chicken marsala, naturally raised beef, or sushi Italiano. Besides, where else in Boston can you get a free luxury sedan service to and from your home, office, or hotel? Open until 11 P.M.

MAP 1 C4 R 4 111 N. WASHINGTON ST. 617-742-2998 WWW.GVANNIS.COM

LEGAL SEA FOODS *BUSINESS • SEAFOOD $$*

Offering the largest selection of freshwater and saltwater fish in town, this East Coast chain has locals swearing by its clam chowder. This nautically themed location is a block from the waterfront.

MAP 1 F5 R 55 255 STATE ST. 617-227-3115 WWW.LEGALSEAFOODS.COM

MAMMA MARIA *HOT SPOT • ITALIAN $$$*

Request a seat at the relatively unknown Table 99, the most romantic spot on the second floor. The seasonal menu exudes rustic charm with offerings like spring lamb in sage butter.

MAP 1 D5 R 23 3 NORTH SQUARE 617-523-0077 WWW.MAMMAMARIA.COM

MIKE'S PASTRY *CAFÉ • ITALIAN $*

The overwhelming scent of fresh cannoli wafts throughout this popular bakery. Table service is available for those looking for a cup of rich coffee served with a rock-candy lollipop.

MAP 1 D4 R 17 300 HANOVER ST. 617-742-3050 WWW.MIKESPASTRY.COM

NEBO *AFTER HOURS • ITALIAN $$*

Named after its North End Boston location, Nebo serves gourmet pizzas and hand-cut pastas to such regulars as Aerosmith's

HANOVER STREET

Walk down the main drag of Hanover Street and it's difficult to resist the doorways of candlelit trattorias and cafés, where the smells of simmering marinara sauce and garlic waft from the kitchens and old men linger over grappa and espresso. Welcome to Boston's version of Little Italy and one of the oldest neighborhoods in town. Since the 1920s, Italians and Italian American culture have dominated here. Nearly 90 restaurants, carryout kitchens, pizzerias, and cozy dining rooms call this neighborhood home and offer consistently good cuisine. There are Thai and Chinese restaurants here, but Hanover Street is most noted for its regional Italian cuisine and impressive selections of Italian wines. Revel in the Italian conversations overheard on outdoor patios and relax with a walk down the narrow streets, which provide sneak peeks at hidden courtyards and beautiful gardens. Some mandatory stops are **Strega (p. 21)** for dinner and **Mike's Pastry (p. 19)** for dessert.

Steven Tyler. With its proximity to TD Banknorth Garden, Nebo also brings in pre- and post-game crowds. Open until midnight Monday–Wednesday and 2 A.M. Thursday–Saturday.

MAP 1 C3 R 3 90 N. WASHINGTON ST.
617-723-6326 WWW.NEBOPIZZERIA.COM

NEPTUNE OYSTER *HOT SPOT • SEAFOOD $$$*
With seating for only about 35, this inventive seafood house packs in a lot of character with mirrors, marble, and red leather. Raw bar fare is typical, but the Italian-accented seafood yields can't-miss offerings.

MAP 1 D4 R 13 63 SALEM ST.
617-742-3474 WWW.NEPTUNEOYSTER.COM

PIZZERIA REGINA *QUICK BITE • ITALIAN $$*
This old-time parlor with wooden booths and a good-naturedly brusque staff is *the* place to go for "wicked awesome" Neapolitan pies. After 80 years, the parlor still succeeds in serving crunchy, chewy, perfect slices.

MAP 1 D4 R 9 11 1/2 THATCHER ST.
617-227-0765 WWW.PIZZERIAREGINA.COM

PREZZA *HOT SPOT • ITALIAN $$$*
The sophisticated crowd orders wood-grilled meats and fish from the inventive Italian menu. Although it may be one of the most expensive restaurants in the North End, foodies marvel at the quality ingredients and exceptional server knowledge.

MAP 1 D5 R 24 24 FLEET ST.
617-227-1577 WWW.PREZZA.COM

SEL DE LA TERRE *BUSINESS • FRENCH $$$*
Cuisine from southern France, rustic earth tones, and a location near the waterfront set the scene for a quiet conversation at lunch, brunch, or dinner.

MAP 1 F5 Ⓡ56 255 STATE ST.
617-720-1300 WWW.SELDELATERRE.COM

STREGA *HOT SPOT • ITALIAN $$$*
With celebrity sightings, movies such as *The Godfather* playing in the background, and stylish servers, the Strega experience does not come cheap. However, entrées such as *costata ripiena* (prosciutto-stuffed veal chops) make for an unforgettable experience.

MAP 1 D5 Ⓡ21 379 HANOVER ST.
617-523-8481 WWW.STREGARISTORANTE.COM

TRESCA *ROMANTIC • ITALIAN $$$*
Co-owned by former Bruin Ray Bourque, Tresca (Italian for "intrigue") offers an all-Italian wine list, handmade pastas, and a four-course tasting menu of regional specialties. The balcony's table for two is the perfect spot for sharing a cognac custard.

MAP 1 E4 Ⓡ32 233 HANOVER ST.
617-742-8240 WWW.TRESCANORTHEND.COM

UNION OYSTER HOUSE *BUSINESS • SEAFOOD $$*
America's oldest restaurant, and where the toothpick was first used, turned 180 in 2006. The multilevel eatery hosts a fabulous oyster bar and dishes New England favorites like lobster ravioli.

MAP 1 E3 Ⓡ27 41 UNION ST.
617-227-2750 WWW.UNIONOYSTERHOUSE.COM

VOLLE NOLLE *BREAKFAST AND BRUNCH • NEW AMERICAN $*
You won't see traditional breakfast items on the menu here but you will find pressed ham and cheese sandwiches. Volle Nolle focuses on comfort food with a healthy twist.

MAP 1 D5 Ⓡ22 351 HANOVER ST.
617-523-0003

MAP 2 BEACON HILL

ARTÚ *QUICK BITE • ITALIAN $$*
Brick walls, an open kitchen, and rolling rotisseries churn out reasonably priced traditional Italian favorites, including lasagna, eggplant parmigiana, and roasted pork loin. The Beacon Hill location is a spin-off of a North End eatery.

MAP 2 E3 Ⓡ15 89 CHARLES ST.
617-227-9023 WWW.ARTUBOSTON.COM

BEACON HILL BISTRO *BUSINESS • FRENCH $$*
Serene enough for a business meal at breakfast, lunch, or dinner, the restaurant at the Beacon Hill Hotel offers a French bistro menu with favorites such as salmon with panko-crusted asparagus and steak frites.

MAP 2 F3 Ⓡ33 25 CHARLES ST.
617-723-1133 WWW.BEACONHILLHOTEL.COM

NEW ENGLAND CUISINE

A trip to this city would be remiss without a sampling of "wicked good" Boston baked beans. **Durgin-Park (p. 18)** serves them up the traditional way, in stone crocks. Bostonians will tell you **Legal Sea Foods (p. 19)** serves up the best clam chowder, but don't ask for the red Manhattan chowder – the creamy New England-style chowder is the declared winner. Must have something to do with that whole New York/Boston rivalry. Local quahogs, hard-shell clams, are delicious served raw or baked and stuffed. Finish up with a slice of Boston cream pie, the official Massachusetts state dessert.

CAFÉ VANILLE *CAFÉ • FRENCH* $

Exquisite petits fours, croissants, donuts, and sandwiches at this French bakery and café will satiate any craving. In the summer, be sure to nab a seat outside on the tiny patio.

MAP 2 E3 R 18 70 CHARLES ST.
617-523-9200 WWW.CAFEVANILLEBOSTON.COM

DANTE *HOT SPOT • MEDITERRANEAN* $$$

Ambitious chef/owner Dante de Magistris of Blu Restaurant fame opened this newcomer in the former Davio's space at the Royal Sonesta Hotel. Dante's Mediterranean-inspired cuisine includes inventive tasting appetizers, raw-bar concoctions, and robust entrées.

MAP 2 A4 R 3 5 CAMBRIDGE PKWY.
617-497-4200 WWW.RESTAURANTDANTE.COM

THE FEDERALIST *BUSINESS • NEW AMERICAN* $$$

Located in the lavish XV Beacon hotel, the Fed commands the power-dining scene with elaborate steaks and chops. Large meetings are held in the wine cellar, where guests ogle a 1907 selection rescued from a schooner.

MAP 2 F6 R 41 15 BEACON ST.
617-670-2515 WWW.XVBEACON.COM/DINING.HTM

FIGS *QUICK BITE • ITALIAN* $$

Celebrity chef Todd English's vision of a gourmet pizzeria churns out flavorful toppings such as fig, prosciutto, and white clam. This 30-seat storefront also has a small selection of creative salads and pastas.

MAP 2 F3 R 30 42 CHARLES ST.
617-742-3447
WWW.TODDENGLISH.COM/RESTAURANTS/FIGS.HTML

LALA ROKH *ROMANTIC • PERSIAN* $$

An exotic blend of Persian spices, fruits, and nuts is served up in this cozy hideaway. Meats and rice are the focus, and if you are unfamiliar with the cuisine, the helpful staff is happy to assist.

MAP 2 E4 R 19 97 MT. VERNON ST.
617-720-5511 WWW.LALAROKH.COM

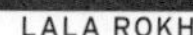

LALA ROKH THE PARAMOUNT PIERROT BISTROT FRANÇAISE

THE PARAMOUNT *QUICK BITE • AMERICAN $$*
This modern coffee shop with exposed brick walls turns more highbrow at night, when you might find pan-seared diver scallops. By day, the cafeteria-style shop dishes up bacon and eggs, pancakes, and burgers.

 F3 R 27 44 CHARLES ST.
617-720-1152 WWW.PARAMOUNTBOSTON.COM

PIERROT BISTROT FRANÇAISE *ROMANTIC • FRENCH $$$*
A largely native French staff serves up ample portions of such classic bistro fare as duck confit, steak tartare, and mussels in white wine. A three-course prix fixe menu is also available.

 D4 R 7 272 CAMBRIDGE ST.
617-725-8855 WWW.PIERROTBISTROT.COM

75 CHESTNUT *ROMANTIC • AMERICAN $$$*
The converted townhouse has become one of the city's top dining destinations serving upscale American bistro-style cuisine. The elegant atmosphere offers a taste of old Boston in a seemingly private club.

 F3 R 29 75 CHESTNUT ST.
617-227-2175 WWW.75CHESTNUT.COM

THE UPPER CRUST *QUICK BITE • ITALIAN $*
Beacon Hill's most upscale pizzeria offers specialty pies with innovative gourmet toppings. Though it might be difficult to get a seat here, this pizza shop also offers carryout and free local delivery service.

 F3 R 37 20 CHARLES ST.
617-723-9600 WWW.THEUPPERCRUSTPIZZERIA.COM

MAP 3 DOWNTOWN/CHINATOWN

AUJOURD'HUI *BUSINESS • NEW AMERICAN-FRENCH $$$*
Haute New American-French cuisine is served here with million-dollar views overlooking the Public Garden. Often touted as the city's best place to dine, suits of all stripes – and celebs, too – come here for power-meal central.

 B1 R 19 FOUR SEASONS HOTEL, 200 BOYLSTON ST.
617-351-2071 WWW.FOURSEASONS.COM

THE BARKING CRAB *QUICK BITE • SEAFOOD $$*

Once just a summer restaurant, this casual, funky New England seafood shack has become a year-round staple. Stick with the fried clams, fish and chips, and other standards.

MAP 3 C6 R 56 88 SLEEPER ST.
617-426-2722 WWW.BARKINGCRAB.COM

CHAU CHOW CITY *BREAKFAST AND BRUNCH • CHINESE $*

This three-level emporium is one of Chinatown's top choices for dim sum. The first two levels showcase seafood, and on weekends dim sum lovers request a third-floor seat to sample *har gau* and *char siu bao.*

MAP 3 C3 R 49 83 ESSEX ST.
617-338-8158

FINALE *CAFÉ • AMERICAN $$*

This desserterie focuses on sweet treats but also offers a good variety of sandwiches and salads. Don't miss the chocolate Temptation for Two that is sure to satisfy any craving.

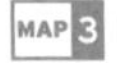
MAP 3 B1 R 20 1 COLUMBUS AVE.
617-423-3184 WWW.FINALEDESSERTS.COM

GINZA *AFTER HOURS • JAPANESE $$*

Sushi seekers come until 3:30 A.M. to this bustling Japanese eatery that specializes in innovative *maki,* hot pot, teriyaki, *udon,* and other selections. The real action is at the sushi bar.

MAP 3 C3 R 52 16 HUDSON ST.
617-338-2261 WWW.GINZABOSTON.COM

THE GOOD LIFE *AFTER HOURS • AMERICAN $$*

Located in the heart of Boston's Financial District, the focus here is on comfort food served amid a stunning collection of artwork by local artists. Couples should request a table at the upstairs room for a quieter experience. Open until 2 A.M. Monday-Saturday.

MAP 3 B3 R 34 28 KINGSTON ST.
617-451-2622 WWW.GOODLIFEBOSTON.COM

IVY RESTAURANT *QUICK BITE • NEW AMERICAN $$*

Small plates and affordable cocktails make this an ideal pre-theater stop. Dessert is not on the menu, but this casual, tri-level eatery offers a unique concept by which every bottle of wine costs $26.

MAP 3 B3 R 25 49 TEMPLE ST.
617-451-1416 WWW.IVYRESTAURANTGROUP.COM

LES ZYGOMATES *AFTER HOURS • FRENCH $$$*

Head to this bistro for a moderately priced French meal and glass of wine (70 are offered by the glass). Request a seat on the "Jazz Side" to enjoy a live performance tableside. Open until 1 A.M. Monday-Saturday.

MAP 3 C3 R 53 129 SOUTH ST.
617-542-5108 WWW.WINEBAR.COM

LOCKE-OBER *BUSINESS • NEW AMERICAN $$$*

Request a private chamber on the third floor (seating 2-16), which best exemplifies the restaurant's rich history. Dine in the prestigious

FINALE

LOCKE-OBER

JFK Room and sample the famed JFK Lobster Stew, named after its biggest fan.

 B3 R 27 3 WINTER PL.
617-542-1340 WWW.LOCKE-OBER.COM

MERITAGE *ROMANTIC • NEW AMERICAN $$$*
Boston Harbor Hotel's incredibly chic restaurant offers arguably the best view of the city from its second floor. Entrées are organized by pairing and matched with flavor. A full-bodied white might be paired with veal sweetbreads.

 B6 R 39 70 ROWES WHARF
617-439-3995 WWW.MERITAGETHERESTAURANT.COM

NO. 9 PARK *HOT SPOT • FRENCH/ITALIAN $$$*
An understated vintage decor allows sophisticated French and Italian dishes to remain center stage. Nearby State House workers come for lunch while serious foodies splurge on the nine-course tasting menu.

 A3 R 4 9 PARK ST.
617-742-9991 WWW.NO9PARK.COM

RADIUS *HOT SPOT • NEW AMERICAN/FRENCH $$$*
You can hear the money talking at this sleek Financial District space – one of the city's top tables – where deal-makers and trendsetters huddle over veal, sweetbreads and melted leeks, or other contemporary French-inspired creations.

 C4 R 54 8 HIGH ST.
617-426-1234 WWW.RADIUSRESTAURANT.COM

SHABU-ZEN *ROMANTIC • JAPANESE $$*
Don't come to the city's first shabu-shabu (translates roughly to "swish swish") house for a traditional experience. Here, you cook your own choice meal complete with thin, uncooked meats, seafood, vegetables, and broth, swirled in a hot pot.

 C3 R 51 16 TYLER ST.
617-292-8828 WWW.SHABUZEN.COM

TROQUET *ROMANTIC • FRENCH $$$*
This self-described food and wine boutique is where wine lovers head for contemporary French bistro fare served by a knowledgeable

staff. Wine takes precedence here, and two- and four-ounce tastings make sampling simpler.

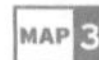
B2 R 22 140 BOYLSTON ST.
617-695-9463 WWW.TROQUETBOSTON.COM

VIA MATTA *HOT SPOT • ITALIAN $$$*
This hip eatery draws a mix of professionals and theatergoers with its inventive Italian cuisine. For larger parties, request the table in the downstairs kitchen and watch celebrity chef Michael Schlow prepare choices as such *pasta e fagioli.*

B1 R 18 79 PARK PLAZA
617-422-0008 WWW.VIAMATTARESTAURANT.COM

MAP 4 BACK BAY/SOUTH END

BARLOLA *QUICK BITE • SPANISH $$*
One of the city's newest Spanish tapas restaurants, located in the basement of an apartment complex, offers a modest menu ideal for sharing. Its tucked-away setting makes it the perfect escape for a quick dish (and sangria) with friends.

B4 R 15 160 COMMONWEALTH AVE.
617-266-1122 WWW.BARLOLA.COM

CAFE JAFFA *CAFÉ • MIDDLE EASTERN $$*
Located off Newbury Street, this Middle Eastern café offers falafel and stuffed grape leaves as well as steak tips, burgers, and a short beer and wine list. It's not fancy, but the prices are surprisingly reasonable.

B3 R 12 48 GLOUCESTER ST.
617-536-0230

DOMANI BAR & TRATTORIA *HOT SPOT • ITALIAN $$*
A young Armani-wearing crowd visits this chic trattoria, which sits above the equally stylish Saint nightclub. In the summer months, grab a seat at the outdoor patio and dine on fettuccine Bolognese.

C4 R 45 51 HUNTINGTON AVE.
617-424-8500 WWW.DOMANIBOSTON.COM

DOUZO *QUICK BITE • JAPANESE $$$*
Modern Japanese cuisine, a minimalist space, and two-story windows make this the place to get your Zen on. With sushi, *maki,* and noodle dishes on the menu, it's the perfect stop for lunch or dinner.

D4 R 62 131 DARTMOUTH ST.
617-859-8885

FLOUR BAKERY + CAFÉ *CAFÉ • AMERICAN $*
Pastries, scones, croissants, and other sweet treats are the specialty at this airy little café. You can get a tasty applewood-smoked bacon sandwich, too, but the homemade Oreo-style cookies steal the spotlight.

F4 R 77 1595 WASHINGTON ST.
617-267-4300 WWW.FLOURBAKERY.COM

FLOUR BAKERY + CAFÉ

L'ESPALIER

THE FRANKLIN CAFÉ *AFTER HOURS • NEW AMERICAN $$*
This moderately priced, cosmopolitan eatery is where chefs off the clock come to dine on comfort food such as smoked pork chops. The cool hangout serves until 1:30 A.M., or come earlier for a quieter experience.

MAP 4 E6 R 76 278 SHAWMUT AVE.
617-350-0010 WWW.FRANKLINCAFE.COM

HAMERSLEY'S BISTRO *BUSINESS • FRENCH-AMERICAN $$$*
The casual setting makes you feel like a dinner guest at a country home but the menu exudes upscale bistro flair. The cassoulet, roast chicken, and other satisfying French-American fare have kept it on many "Boston's best" lists.

MAP 4 E5 R 72 553 TREMONT ST.
617-423-2700 WWW.HAMERSLEYSBISTRO.COM

L'ESPALIER *ROMANTIC • FRENCH $$$*
Situated in a historic Back Bay townhouse, this French classic is one of Boston's most romantic spots. The opulent prix fixe menu will set you back big bucks, but it's the crème de la crème of lasting impressions.

MAP 4 B3 R 8 30 GLOUCESTER ST.
617-262-3023 WWW.LESPALIER.COM

MISTRAL *HOT SPOT • FRENCH-MEDITERRANEAN $$$*
Consistently producing imaginative French-Mediterranean fare, this see-and-be-seen South Ender continues to be all the rage. The city's beautiful crowd congregates in this grand, high-ceilinged room for its popular thin-crust grilled pizzas.

MAP 4 D5 R 56 223 COLUMBUS AVE.
617-867-9300 WWW.MISTRALBISTRO.COM

THE OAK ROOM *ROMANTIC • STEAKHOUSE $$$*
If ever there were such a thing as a luxurious steakhouse, this would be the epitome. Edwardian woodwork, rich colors, refined service, and perfectly seared porterhouses and butter-rich seafood specialties are reasons guests keep returning.

MAP 4 C5 R 51 138 ST. JAMES AVE.
617-267-5300 WWW.THEOAKROOM.COM

THE OTHER SIDE CAFÉ *CAFÉ • VEGETARIAN $*
Artwork from local artists decorates the walls of this hip and

healthy café. The menu features large salads and sandwiches, fresh juice, smoothies, espresso, and a list of imported beers.

MAP 4 B2 R 3 407 NEWBURY ST. AT MASSACHUSETTS AVE.
617-536-9477

THE RED FEZ *AFTER HOURS • MEDITERRANEAN/MIDDLE EASTERN $$*

The legendary Red Fez opened here more than 40 years ago and today serves *mezze* to a new generation of trendy barflies. The hot and cold selections include *zahtar* salad and pan-seared chicken livers. Open until 12 midnight nightly.

MAP 4 F6 R 82 1222 WASHINGTON ST.
617-338-6060 WWW.THEREDFEZ.COM

SIBLING RIVALRY *HOT SPOT • AMERICAN $$$*

The split menu presents two brothers' unique takes on appetizers and entrées. The beef selection on Chef David's menu might offer a pan-seared bone-in rib eye, while Chef Bob offers braised short ribs.

MAP 4 E5 R 73 525 TREMONT ST.
617-338-5338 WWW.SIBLINGRIVALRYBOSTON.COM

SONSIE *CAFÉ • NEW AMERICAN $$*

Come in the morning and linger over a coffee and pastry, or dine in the evening among Boston's beautiful Prada-clad crowd. The kitchen is successful in turning out New American fare such as pizza with chicken and jack cheese.

MAP 4 B2 R 4 327 NEWBURY ST.
617-351-2500 WWW.SONSIEBOSTON.COM

SORELLINA *ROMANTIC • ITALIAN $$$*

Chef Jamie Mammano of Mistral and Teatro fame brings the "little sister" (in Italian) to the former Salamander space. Sophisticated yet casual Italian fare and fun, flirty cocktails are what Sorellina is all about.

MAP 4 C4 R 44 1 HUNTINGTON AVE.
617-412-4600 WWW.SORELLINABOSTON.COM

STELLA *HOT SPOT • ITALIAN $$$*

Due to its chic decor, trendy location, and reasonably priced menu of Italian favorites, Stella has become one of the hippest eateries in town. Locals and out-of-towners alike come for the pasta Bolognese and roasted duck.

MAP 4 F4 R 78 1525 WASHINGTON ST.
617-247-7747 WWW.BOSTONSTELLA.COM

STEPHANIE'S ON NEWBURY *BREAKFAST AND BRUNCH • NEW AMERICAN $$*

The focus here is on comfort – from sinfully rich macaroni and cheese to the plush, luxe booths. Request a table at the outdoor patio where the people-watching scene is worth the sometimes-lengthy wait.

MAP 4 B4 R 17 190 NEWBURY ST.
617-236-0990 WWW.STEPHANIESONNEWBURY.COM

TOP OF THE HUB *ROMANTIC • NEW AMERICAN $$$*

For the most encompassing city views, visit the Prudential

SORELLINA

28 DEGREES

Center's 52nd floor for a memorable evening. New American entrées include a macadamia-crusted tuna steak. Keep the night alive with after-dinner drinks at the bar.

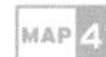 C3 Ⓡ38 800 BOYLSTON ST.
617-536-1775 WWW.TOPOFTHEHUB.NET

TREMONT 647 *HOT SPOT • NEW AMERICAN $$$*
This South End hot spot is known for its weekend pajama brunches, where the staff – and uninhibited diners – roll out of bed and to the breakfast table. The dinner menu offers comfort food with a creative flare.

 E4 Ⓡ70 647 TREMONT ST.
617-266-4600 WWW.TREMONT647.COM

28 DEGREES *HOT SPOT • NEW AMERICAN $$*
Named after the temperature at which the perfect martini should be served, this fanciful eatery serves 28 stylish plates designed to be shared among good company.

 D6 Ⓡ67 1 APPLETON ST.
617-728-0728 WWW.28DEGREES-BOSTON.COM

UNION BAR & GRILLE *HOT SPOT • AMERICAN $$*
Enter the sleek dining room where fashionistas congregate in circular black banquettes. There's even a $10K tuna steak on the menu, named after a contest in which the chef's spice rub won $10K.

MAP 4 F5 Ⓡ79 1357 WASHINGTON ST.
617-423-0555 WWW.UNIONRESTAURANT.COM

MAP 5 FENWAY/KENMORE SQUARE

BROWN SUGAR CAFÉ *QUICK BITE • THAI $*
The reasonably priced Thai food includes basics like curries and pad thai – and more exotic specialties, such as spicy, crispy watercress and golden bags of filled tofu skin. Every table is given a jar of brown sugar.

 E4 Ⓡ31 129 JERSEY ST.
617-266-2928 WWW.BROWNSUGARCAFE.COM

CLIO *HOT SPOT • FRENCH-AMERICAN $$$*

The intensively innovative menu at this chic and ever so pricey Eliot Hotel dining room boasts French-American cuisine. Sushi lovers also flock to Uni, the adjacent sashimi bar.

MAP 5 D6 R 29 370 COMMONWEALTH AVE. 617-536-7200 WWW.CLIORESTAURANT.COM

EASTERN STANDARD *AFTER HOURS • FRENCH $$$*

At this Hotel Commonwealth dining room, the French country menu includes steak frites and other classic fare. Enjoy a seat on the square's largest outdoor patio, where you can catch Red Sox fans heading to a nearby game. Open until midnight Sunday-Thursday and 1 A.M. Friday-Saturday.

MAP 5 C5 R 8 528 COMMONWEALTH AVE. 617-532-9100 WWW.HOTELCOMMONWEALTH.COM

EL PELON TAQUERIA *QUICK BITE • MEXICAN $*

This small, colorful restaurant offers alfresco dining and is well known for its overstuffed *carnitas* burritos, fish tacos, and other authentic south-of-the-border bites.

MAP 5 D4 R 25 92 PETERBOROUGH ST. 617-262-9090 WWW.ELPELON.COM

GAME ON! SPORTS CAFE *QUICK BITE • AMERICAN $*

Grab a burger at "the official bar of any game that's on." This former bowling alley space is now a modern restaurant that caters to the sports fanatic with 90 plasma and high definition TVs.

MAP 5 C4 R 6 82 LANSDOWNE ST. 617-351-7001 WWW.GAMEONBOSTON.COM

THE GARDNER CAFÉ *CAFÉ • FRENCH-AMERICAN $$*

An oasis in the Isabella Stewart Gardner Museum, this cozy lunch-only café pleases art patrons with a small yet sophisticated menu of light, French-accented fare. Choices might run from salads and pâté to quiche and lamb *tagine*.

MAP 5 F3 R 35 280 THE FENWAY 617-566-1088 WWW.GARDNERMUSEUM.ORG

GREAT BAY *ROMANTIC • SEAFOOD $$$*

Sophisticated seafood, like pan-seared Kona snapper, has turned this elegant hotel restaurant into a trendy destination. At the eatery's Island bar, patrons dine on ceviches, oysters, and innovative salads.

MAP 5 C5 R 16 500 COMMONWEALTH AVE. 617-532-5300 WWW.GREATBAYRESTAURANT.COM

LINWOOD BAR AND GRILL *QUICK BITE • BARBECUE $*

The menu offers slow-cooked St. Louis-style barbecue ribs and Southern favorites such as catfish fingers. Its off-the-beaten-path location is ideal prior to or after a Sox game to avoid the area's packed restaurants.

MAP 5 E4 R 30 81 KILMARNOCK ST. 617-247-8099 WWW.LINWOODGRILL.COM

SORENTO'S *QUICK BITE • ITALIAN $$*
If you are looking for something more than just a hot dog before a Red Sox game, Sorento's reasonably priced menu of Italian dishes is a satisfying option. Faithful regulars return for favorites such as pizza, pasta, and homemade cannoli.

MAP 5 D4 R 23 86 PETERBOROUGH ST.
617-424-7070 WWW.SORENTOS.COM

MAP 6 CAMBRIDGE/HARVARD SQUARE

BOLOCO *QUICK BITE • MEXICAN $*
It doesn't get any better than enormous burritos for $6, mango smoothies, and wraps on the go. Choose from more than a dozen menu items or build your own from chicken, steak, tofu, shrimp, or roasted vegetables.

MAP 6 E3 R 43 71 MT. AUBURN ST.
617-354-5838 WWW.INSPIREDBURRITOS.COM

CRAIGIE STREET BISTROT *ROMANTIC • FRENCH $$$*
Tucked into an underground space outside of Harvard Square, this French restaurant is decorated with Parisian postcards, cookbooks, and other collectibles. The menu changes daily to include fresh ingredients, but comes at hefty prices.

MAP 6 A2 R 1 5 CRAIGIE CIR.
617-497-5511 WWW.CRAIGIESTREETBISTROT.COM

HARVEST *BREAKFAST AND BRUNCH • AMERICAN $$$*
Eat in the peaceful dining room or request a seat in the square's only outdoor café. The three-course, prix fixe Sunday brunch includes items like chilled gazpacho with crabmeat and an open-faced omelet with tomato leek fondue.

MAP 6 C2 R 7 44 BRATTLE ST.
617-868-2255 WWW.HARVESTCAMBRIDGE.COM

HENRIETTA'S TABLE *HOT SPOT • AMERICAN $$*
Enjoy fresh seasonal meals and a casual dining experience for breakfast, lunch, or dinner. Local New England products make up the menu, which offers plenty of options for vegetarians and carnivores alike.

MAP 6 D2 R 15 CHARLES HOTEL, 1 BENNETT ST.
617-661-5005 WWW.HENRIETTASTABLE.COM

MR. BARTLEY'S BURGER COTTAGE *QUICK BITE • AMERICAN $*
Cheap, fast, and undeniably the best burger joint in town, this small cottage pumps out thick, juicy burgers and artery-clogging onion rings. The down-and-dirty landmark has been a beloved student hangout since the early '60s.

MAP 6 E4 R 48 1246 MASSACHUSETTS AVE.
617-354-6559 WWW.MRBARTLEY.COM

OM *ROMANTIC • NEW AMERICAN $$$*
Rachel Klein (formerly of XO Café and Lot 41 in Providence) takes Cambridge by surprise with her creative fusion of American classics

RIALTO

UPSTAIRS ON THE SQUARE

and Southeast Asian seasonings. Don't miss her filet mignon and fried truffle egg entrée.

MAP 6 D3 R 31 92 WINTHROP ST. 617-576-2800 WWW.OMRESTAURANT.COM

RIALTO *BUSINESS • MEDITERRANEAN $$$*
Jody Adams, one of the area's most acclaimed chefs, has defined Mediterranean cuisine. Her pan-roasted veal chops are served up in style at this airy dining room at the Charles Hotel overlooking Harvard Square.

MAP 6 D2 R 14 CHARLES HOTEL, 1 BENNETT ST. 617-661-5050 WWW.RIALTO-RESTAURANT.COM

UPSTAIRS ON THE SQUARE *HOT SPOT • NEW AMERICAN $$$*
It's a soiree every night at this Alice-in-Wonderland fantasy where pink plaid walls, animal-print carpeting, and eye-catching chandeliers are the hallmark. Visitors enjoy the tasting menu of items such as soft-shell crab tempura and lemongrass-steamed yellow snapper. Vegetarians also will not be disappointed.

MAP 6 D2 R 19 91 WINTHROP ST. 617-864-1933 WWW.UPSTAIRSONTHESQUARE.COM

C VEGGIE PLANET *QUICK BITE • VEGETARIAN $*
These basement digs at venerable folk-music venue Club Passim won't win any design prizes, but this earthy pizzeria serves high-quality vegetarian fare. Besides the signature pies, there are salads, soups, and rice plates.

MAP 6 D3 R 26 47 PALMER ST. 617-661-1513 WWW.VEGGIEPLANET.NET

OVERVIEW MAP

CHEZ HENRI *HOT SPOT • FRENCH $$$*
This sultry bistro provides elbow-patched professors and Cambridge hipsters with red banquettes where French fare is spiced up with Cuban flavors – think coriander, plantains, and pork. At night, there is a three-course prix fixe menu as well.

OVERVIEW MAP B2 1 SHEPARD ST. 617-354-8980 WWW.CHEZHENRI.COM

NIGHTLIFE

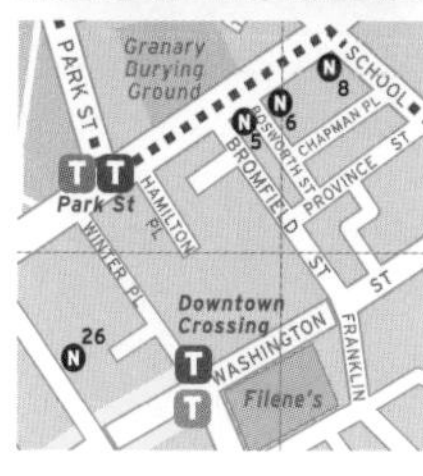

Most historic tavern: **GREEN DRAGON,** p. 34

Where to hear the strongest Boston accent: **HENNESSY'S,** p. 34

Best chance for a local celebrity sighting: **VERTIGO LOUNGE,** p. 35

Best signature cocktails: **LUCKY'S LOUNGE,** p. 37

Best beer selection: **BUKOWSKI TAVERN,** p. 38

Classiest hotel bar: **THE OAK BAR,** p. 39

Best bar to talk about logarithms and play chess: **SHAY'S PUB AND WINE BAR,** p. 42

MAP 1 NORTH END/GOVERNMENT CENTER

THE BLACK ROSE *PUB*

A family-owned Irish pub, the Rose is well loved by Boston visitors and Irish emigrants searching for an authentic touch of green. A reliable pint of Guinness comes with a side of live Irish music.

MAP 1 F4 N 51 160 STATE ST.
617-742-2286 WWW.IRISHCONNECTION.COM

GREEN DRAGON *PUB*

This historic pub touts itself as the "headquarters of the Revolution," where patriots met to talk rebellion. Today, it's a convivial Irish hangout favored by expats.

MAP 1 E3 N 26 11 MARSHALL ST.
617-367-0055 WWW.SOMERSPUBS.COM

HENNESSY'S *PUB*

You'll hear plenty of "Bawstin" accents at this modern Irish pub set along the Freedom Trail. Equipped with a coal fireplace for winter evenings and open sidewalk windows for summer people-watching, Hennessy's is a Boston mainstay.

MAP 1 E3 N 28 25 UNION ST.
617-742-2121 WWW.SOMERSPUBS.COM

THE LIVING ROOM *LOUNGE*

The Living Room features plush couches to sink into while you sip your martini. Its out-of-the-way location tends to attract a mellow crowd of young professionals.

MAP 1 F5 N 53 101 ATLANTIC AVE.
617-723-5101 WWW.LIVINGROOMBOSTON.COM

IRISH PUBS

Thank the Irish immigrants for allowing Bostonians to enjoy some of the best Irish pubs in the country. **Hennessy's (p. 34)** is a "wicked killa" bar by the standards of most Irish expats. **The Black Rose (p. 34),** named after the 17th-century idyllic poem *Roisin Dubh* (the small black rose), has live Irish music every night and serves traditional Irish fare. It is said that Paul Revere and the Sons of Liberty favored the **Green Dragon (p. 34)** as a meeting spot when planning the Boston Tea Party in 1773. Today's tavern is a reconstruction of the original. Boston is brimming with authentic Irish spots to enjoy a Guinness or Irish whiskey in the company of strong accents. The website www.bostonirishpubs.com lists some of the best Irish nightlife and events in the city.

HENNESSY'S

PARRIS

PARRIS *DANCE CLUB*

This cavernous dance hall features sweeping, oddly shaped furniture to catch you when you tire of dancing. The music is an eclectic blend of Top 40 and cocktail jazz.

MAP 1 F4 N 48 250 QUINCY MARKET BUILDING, 2ND FL.
617-248-9900 WWW.PARRISBOSTON.COM

THE RUBY ROOM *LOUNGE*

This beautiful hotel bar is the only lounge atmosphere in the sports-heavy North End. There are no TV screens here. Instead you'll find unique cocktails like the Mango Tango made with mango vodka and muddled basil.

MAP 1 D2 N 8 155 PORTLAND ST.
617-557-9950 WWW.RUBYROOMBOSTON.COM

STANZA DEI SIGARI *CIGAR BAR*

A former speakeasy from the 1920s, this cigar bar boasts an impressive selection of cigars, bourbon, cognac, and single-malt scotch. Enjoy a stogie and the cozy antique decor with local old-timers.

MAP 1 D4 N 16 292 HANOVER ST.
617-227-0295 WWW.STANZADEISIGARI.COM

VERTIGO LOUNGE *DANCE CLUB*

Chill out in the stylish lounge or head downstairs to find DJs spinning everything from hip-hop to Haitian music. You are sure to see some of the music industry's hottest local celebs.

MAP 1 F3 N 44 126 STATE ST.
617-723-7277

MAP 2 BEACON HILL

CHEERS *PUB*

Don't be disappointed if you don't see Norm here. The bar that inspired the TV show *Cheers* looks nothing like the sitcom set. Lift a pint and toast Sam, Diane, Carla, and the clan anyway.

F3 N 34 84 BEACON ST.
617-227-9605 WWW.CHEERSBOSTON.COM

HARVARD GARDENS *BAR*

This airy upscale bar comes furnished with tablecloths and an inventive drink menu. The young blue-blazer/pearl-necklace clientele lets its hair down after midnight.

 6 316 CAMBRIDGE ST.
617-523-2727 WWW.HARVARDGARDENS.COM

THE SEVENS *BAR*

Slip into a wooden booth, order a pint of something frosty, and start making new friends. Beacon Hill kicks back at this casual neighborhood bar that draws Brahmins and bohemians alike.

 17 77 CHARLES ST.
617-523-9074

6B *LOUNGE*

Catering to the local after-work crowd, this place gets more hoppin' each hour into the night. The drink menu, filled with innovative martinis, changes weekly. Try a concoction with pomegranate, pear, or mango juice.

 43 6 BEACON ST.
617-742-0306

21ST AMENDMENT *PUB*

Named after the law ending Prohibition, this historic pub is your best bet for picking up local political gossip. State House politicos crowd the notched wooden tables to consume drinks like Pete's Perilous Punch and to trade favors.

 40 150 BOWDOIN ST.
617-227-7100 WWW.21STBOSTON.COM

MAP 3 DOWNTOWN/CHINATOWN

BEANTOWN PUB *PUB*

Across from the Granary Burying Ground, Beantown Pub is the only place you can drink a Sam Adams beer within sight of Samuel Adams's grave. The tiled floor and marble counters add class to this neighborhood beer garden.

 6 100 TREMONT ST.
617-426-0111 WWW.BEANTOWNPUB.COM

THE BLACK RHINO *BAR/PUB*

A mix of bankers, brokers, and lawyers usually stocks this downtown bar. The business-casual ambience and decor make it a great place for an after-work pint and calamari.

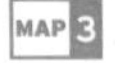 12 21 BROAD ST.
617-263-0101 WWW.THEBLACKRHINO.COM

CAPRICE/UNDERBAR *LOUNGE/DANCE CLUB*

The perfect place for a post-theater drink, Caprice is a giant, chill lounge with a dull murmur of conversation. Underbar, downstairs, is one of Boston's hippest Manhattan-esque nightclubs.

 47 275 TREMONT ST.
617-292-0080 WWW.ROXYBOSTON.COM

FELT

LUCKY'S LOUNGE

FELT *POOL HALL/DANCE CLUB*
This swanky four-level pool hall and club seems to come from Transylvania by way of Neptune. Marble stairs lead to a high-ceilinged room furnished with intergalactic furniture. Local celebs and pseudo-celebs are known to pass by.

 533 WASHINGTON ST.
617-350-5555 WWW.FELTBOSTON.COM

LAST HURRAH *PUB*
The photos on the wall of this old-world hotel bar pay homage to the city's Irish Catholic political past. Try the Liquid Boston Creme Pie, a glorified White Russian.

 60 SCHOOL ST.
617-227-8600

LUCKY'S LOUNGE *LOUNGE*
It's worth the walk over the bridge to this present-day speakeasy. This retro Rat Pack bar has no sign out front, but it offers live music and signature drinks like pomegranate and espresso martinis.

 355 CONGRESS ST.
617-357-5825 WWW.LUCKYSLOUNGE.COM

OM BAR *LOUNGE*
The neon blue light rods look like bug zappers, but they only attract beautiful nightcrawlers to this lounge located in a former bank vault. See and be seen to a soundtrack of thundering trance.

 52 TEMPLE PL.
617-542-8111
WWW.MANTRARESTAURANT.COM/OMBAR.HTML

THE ROXY *DANCE CLUB*
A most elegant space, The Roxy re-creates an early 20th-century ballroom with a 360-degree balcony overlooking the dance floor. As an anything-goes dance palace, it also books local and national bands.

 279 TREMONT ST.
617-338-7699 WWW.ROXYBOSTON.COM

SILVERTONE BAR AND GRILL *PUB*
How many bars can say they make their own raspberry vodka? Silvertone does, and the raspberry martini is highly recommended. Reasonably priced wines keep the local after-work crowd happy.

 69 BROMFIELD ST.
617-338-7887

BACK BAY/SOUTH END

BAR 10 *LOUNGE*

A quiet, chic place to nosh after work or begin a night out, the Westin's dimly lit Bar 10 features comfy divans, shareable appetizers, and generous martinis.

 C4 **47** 10 HUNTINGTON AVE. 617-424-7446

BUKOWSKI TAVERN *PUB*

This friendly little bar named after the author offers more than 100 beers, with a menu explaining the brewing styles of each. The $1.69 hot dogs and hamburgers are served until 8 P.M. Ask about the "Dead Author's Club."

 C2 **36** 50 DALTON ST. 617-437-9999

THE BUTCHER SHOP *WINE BAR*

This artsy, cozy wine bar also houses an upscale butcher shop and restaurant. Enjoy a glass of fine wine or beer while gazing at beautiful cuts of meats and cheeses or the attractive passersby.

 E5 **74** 552 TREMONT STREET 617-423-4800 WWW.THEBUTCHERSHOPBOSTON.COM

CITY BAR *LOUNGE*

The quintessential hotel bar, this hidden gem is sexy, comfortable, and dark enough for a serious conversation or a surreptitious tryst. Enigmatic photos of Victorian women watch over the room.

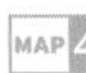 C4 **42** 61 EXETER ST. 617-536-5300 WWW.CITYBARBOSTON.COM

CLUB CAFÉ *QUEER/LOUNGE*

The hub of Boston's gay and lesbian scene, this well-lit bar draws a gregarious crowd who trades gossip before and after clubbing. Don't be surprised if you are drawn into a conversation at the next table.

 C5 **55** 209 COLUMBUS AVE. 617-536-0966 WWW.CLUBCAFE.COM

DELUX CAFÉ AND LOUNGE *BAR*

At this refreshingly relaxed find in this trendy neighborhood, you'll find album covers, Christmas lights, and Elvis paraphernalia on the walls. Bike messengers and businessmen alike down pints while watching the Cartoon Network.

 D5 **64** 100 CHANDLER ST. 617-338-5258

FRITZ *QUEER*

Dubbed "Boston's Gay Sports Bar," Fritz is a popular spot for knocking back a few drinks and watching the home team on plasma TVs. Sunday afternoons are best, when friendly patrons wind up the weekend.

 D6 **66** 26 CHANDLER ST. 617-482-4428 WWW.FRITZBOSTON.COM

BUKOWSKI TAVERN THE BUTCHER SHOP

MATCH LOUNGE *LOUNGE*
The dimly lit, sleek lounge next to the Match restaurant serves a Mango Schizzle (mango schnapps, raspberry vodka, pineapple juice, and chambord) and the restaurant's signature mini burgers.

 B2 N 2 94 MASSACHUSETTS AVE.
617-247-9922 WWW.MATCHBACKBAY.COM

THE OAK BAR *LOUNGE*
The whirring ceiling fans and portraits of gentlemen here recall a scene out of a Rudyard Kipling poem. Service is beyond reproach, as is the selection of single malts, in this "Best of Boston" hotel bar.

 C5 N 51 138 ST. JAMES AVE.
617-267-5300

WHISKEY PARK *LOUNGE*
With faux-fur couches, a candlelit room, and patrons wielding top-shelf cocktails, this sleek hotel bar is the brainchild of nightlife impresario Rande Gerber.

 C6 N 59 64 ARLINGTON ST.
617-542-1483 WWW.BOSTONPARKPLAZA.COM

MAP 5 FENWAY/KENMORE SQUARE

AVALON *DANCE CLUB*
Silk shirts and short skirts are the dress code of choice at the city's most popular dance club. The high-energy room spares no expense on lights, smoke, and the hottest national and international DJs.

 D5 N 26 15 LANSDOWNE ST.
617-262-2424 WWW.AVALONBOSTON.COM

AXIS *DANCE CLUB*
Kid brother to Avalon, this over-the-top dance club draws an edgier crowd with specialty evenings featuring alternative music, cult DJs, and the city's best gay dance night.

 D5 N 27 13 LANSDOWNE ST.
617-262-2437 WWW.BOSTONAXIS.COM

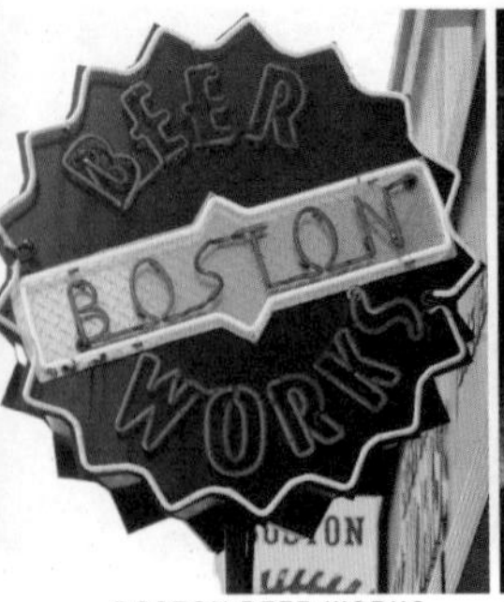

BOSTON BEER WORKS CASK'N FLAGON

BOSTON BEER WORKS *PUB*

The scent of brewing hops fills this cavernous, copper-plated church of beer. Filled to capacity before and after Red Sox games, it's perfect for group outings off-season.

 61 BROOKLINE AVE.
617-536-2337 WWW.BEERWORKS.NET

BOSTON BILLIARD CLUB *POOL HALL*

A classic pool hall, the BBC has a decor straight out of a game of Clue. Finish your game before you plunge into the potent menu of specialty drinks like the cognac martini and Lustful Kiss.

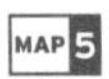 126 BROOKLINE AVE.
617-536-7665 WWW.BOSTONBILLIARDCLUB.COM

CASK'N FLAGON *SPORTS BAR*

You're guaranteed to see a "Yankees Suck" T-shirt at this pub that caters to Sox fans; it's as much a part of Fenway as the franks. Rebuilt to double its size in 2006, it now holds 65 flat-screen TVs.

 62 BROOKLINE AVE.
617-536-4840 WWW.CASKNFLAGON.COM

THE PARADISE ROCK CLUB *CLUB/LOUNGE*

The Paradise is simply one of the best places in town to catch a live band. The layout is ideal, allowing you to get right up to the stage or hang back on the spacious balcony and schmooze.

 967 COMMONWEALTH AVE.
617-562-8800 WWW.THEDISE.COM

RAMROD/MACHINE *QUEER/DANCE CLUB*

You get two choices at these adjoining gay clubs: leather and denim at Ramrod or club kids and pounding house at Machine.

 1254-1256 BOYLSTON ST.
617-266-2986 WWW.RAMRODBOSTON.COM

MAP 6 CAMBRIDGE/HARVARD SQUARE

GRAFTON STREET *BAR*

You can watch the activity of Harvard Square through the open

CENTRAL SQUARE

Not far from Harvard Square along Massachusetts Avenue in Cambridge, Central Square is less polished than its academic neighbor and is known for its diverse selection of clubs and bars. It's one of the liveliest neighborhoods in the Boston area and is easily accessible from the Red Line T. Its best-known club is **The Middle East** (472-480 Massachusetts Ave., 617-864-3278, www.mideastclub.com), the center of the Boston-area rock scene. **T. T. The Bear's Place** (10 Brookline St., 617-492-0082, www.ttthebears.com) next door is an intimate space for seeing up-and-coming bands. The **People's Republik** (876 Massachusetts Ave., 617-492-8632) offers some unusual microbrews on tap and features Soviet-era posters on the walls. **The Enormous Room** (567 Massachusetts Ave., 617-491-5550, www.enormous.tv) may not offer as much elbow room as its name implies, but it is effortlessly cool with DJs spinning dance music most nights of the week. Look for the sign with the red elephant. For something a little more eclectic, try the **Cantab Lounge** (738 Massachusetts Ave., 617-354-2685, www.cantab-lounge.com), where you can catch a poetry slam, live bluegrass, or the legendary Little Joe Cook.

windows at this modern Irish bar. Grab a few friends and order the signature Grafton Goblet, a mix of Irish spirits and fruit juices that's a twist on the more common Scorpion Bowl.

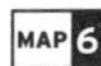 E4 45 1230 MASSACHUSETTS AVE.
617-497-0400 WWW.GRAFTONSTREETCAMBRIDGE.COM

GRENDEL'S DEN *PUB*

This subterranean hangout is popular with Harvard students, who tolerate the notoriously gruff waitstaff. Come for happy hour, when everything on the menu is half price when you buy a drink.

 D2 20 89 WINTHROP ST.
617-491-1160 WWW.GRENDELSDEN.COM

NOIR *LOUNGE*

When this lounge opened up in the Charles Hotel in 2002, it instantly became the new black. The lighting is dim, the vinyl booths are dark, and the drinks are named after film noir icons.

 D2 16 CHARLES HOTEL, 1 BENNETT ST.
617-661-8010 WWW.NOIR-BAR.COM

OM *LOUNGE*

The mixologists at Om's lounge craft cocktails infused with essential oils. Water runs down the walls at this chichi Harvard hangout with a Tibetan theme.

MAP 6 D3 N 31 91 WINTHROP ST.
617-576-2800 WWW.OMRESTAURANT.COM

REDLINE *LOUNGE*

Named after the subway line that runs through Cambridge, this hip hangout is sleek, sexy, and usually packed. It's also got a great bar menu.

MAP 6 E2 N 40 59 JOHN F. KENNEDY ST.
617-491-9851 WWW.REDLINECAMBRIDGE.COM

REGATTABAR *JAZZ CLUB*

You won't find frills or pretensions here – only as many seats as can be crammed into the room, which hosts big-name jazz musicians as they swing through Boston.

MAP 6 D2 N 17 CHARLES HOTEL, 1 BENNETT ST.
617-661-5000 WWW.REGATTABARJAZZ.COM

SHAY'S PUB AND WINE BAR *BAR/PUB*

This is the only bar in Harvard Square with an outdoor patio where you can kick back on a warm day and enjoy a pint. On colder days, have a cider and port with half-price appetizers during happy hour.

MAP 6 E2 N 41 58 JOHN F. KENNEDY ST.
617-864-9161

S SHOPS

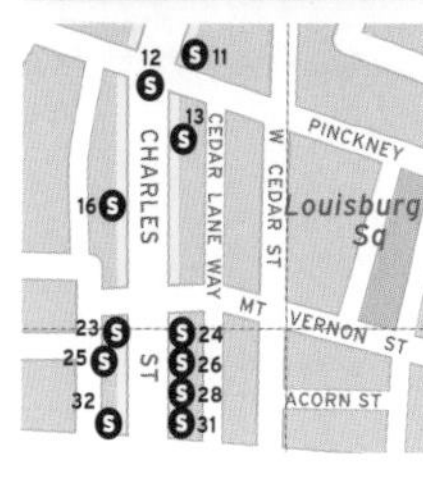

Best threads on a Brahmin budget: **LOUIS BOSTON,** p. 51

Best affordable fashion: **JASMINE SOLA,** p. 51

Best stop for Sox devotees: **THE SOUVENIR STORE,** p. 54

Best oasis for oenophiles: **BRIX,** p. 50

Best beauty escape: **G SPA,** p. 50

Best hip home accessories: **BLISS HOME,** p. 49

Most entertaining tchotchkes: **BLACK INK,** p. 46

Most decadent treats: **TEMPER CHOCOLATES,** p. 55

Best proof that Puritanism is dead: **FRENCH DRESSING,** p. 46

Best place to shop like a New Yorker:
BARNEYS NEW YORK, p. 49

MAP 1 NORTH END/GOVERNMENT CENTER

BOSTON PEWTER COMPANY *GIFT AND HOME*

Revere bowls, baby cups, and candleholders are among the items of inventive metalwork that line the shelves here. Most double as souvenirs and collectors' items.

MAP 1 F4 S 49 FANEUIL HALL, 5 SOUTH MARKET BUILDING, 2ND FL.
617-523-1776 WWW.BOSTONPEWTERCOMPANY.COM

CADIA VINTAGE *GIFT AND HOME*

Open only on weekends or by appointment, this backstreet cubbyhole is a Brigadoon for fans of retro, kitsch, and classic design. Culled from estate sales all over the nation, the wares include vintage Pyrex, 1950s flatware, ceramic geisha bookends, and catwalk-worthy costume jewelry.

MAP 1 D4 S 10 148 SALEM ST.
617-742-1203 WWW.CADIAVINTAGE.COM

CHRISTINA DEFALCO *CLOTHING AND SHOES*

This eponymous shop holds the wares of a designer famed for her fun T-shirts (splashed with Swarovski crystals and depicting images ranging from Audrey Hepburn to Mike's Pastry), funky French cocktail rings, and polyurethane parkas.

MAP 1 D5 S 20 383 HANOVER ST.
617-523-8870 WWW.CHRISTINADEFALCO.COM

DAIRY FRESH CANDIES *GOURMET GOODIES*

One of the North End's most delicious resources has nothing to do with pasta: Dairy Fresh Candies scoops up cavity-worthy sugared grapefruit slices, hazelnut toffee, chocolate-dipped dried fruits, and "gummy everything."

MAP 1 E4 S 30 57 SALEM ST.
617-742-9828 HTTP://DAIRYFRESHCANDIES.COM

FANEUIL HALL/QUINCY MARKET PLACE

See SIGHTS, p. 3.

MAP 1 F3 ✪ 42 4 SOUTH MARKET BUILDING
617-523-1300 WWW.FANEUILHALLMARKETPLACE.COM

HAYMARKET *GOURMET GOODIES*

With tables piled high with fruits, vegetables, and the freshest seafood imaginable, this crowded Friday and Saturday open-air market is a favorite for locals and visitors alike. Just remember, you can touch it only after you buy it.

MAP 1 E4 S 38 BLACKSTONE ST. BTWN NORTH AND HANOVER STS.

INJEANIUS *CLOTHING AND SHOES*

An encyclopedic assortment of denims dominates the racks at this niche boutique, which also stocks casuals, clubwear, and accessories. With labels like Arch Indigo, Rock & Republic, and Hudson, a flattering fit can be found for every form.

MAP 1 D5 S 19 441 HANOVER ST.
617-523-5326

CADIA VINTAGE

SALUMERIA ITALIANA

JOI SALON *BATH, BEAUTY, AND SPA*
The waterfront's electric green Aveda concept salon aims to provide fresh serenity at every turn, with soothing facials, massages, and especially fine pedicures. Haircuts and color are also popular.

 E5 S 40 2 ATLANTIC AVE.
617-723-6330 WWW.JOISALON.COM

KARMA *CLOTHING AND ACCESSORIES*
This North End sister act (owned and operated by twins) upgrades the neighborhood's fashion profile with designer consignments from the likes of Fendi, Prada, Gucci, Dolce & Gabbana, and Versace.

 D4 S 14 26 PRINCE ST.
617-723-8338

MODO GATTO *CLOTHING AND SHOES*
For some men, shopping is its own reward. For others, racks full of Theory, Ben Sherman, and Tavernetti don't stand a chance against a television tuned to local sports. You'll find both at Modo Gatto, the North End's newest outpost for metrosexual threads.

 D5 S 18 424 HANOVER ST.
617-523-4286

MUSEUM OF FINE ARTS BOSTON GIFT SHOP *GIFT AND HOME*
The MFA's coveted art collections are the inspiration for the wares at its off-site boutique. Find Degas mugs, print reproductions, Renoir fridge magnets, plus jewelry and cards.

 F4 S 50 FANEUIL HALL, 3 SOUTH MARKET BUILDING
617-720-1266 WWW.MFASHOP.COM

RAND MCNALLY MAP AND TRAVEL *BOOKS AND MUSIC*
With walls of international and domestic maps and a sizable stock of travel books, Rand McNally is perfect for feeding wanderlust.

 F3 S 43 84 STATE ST.
617-720-1125 WWW.RANDMCNALLY.COM

SALUMERIA ITALIANA *GOURMET GOODIES*
Imported cheeses, cured meats, bags upon bags of specialty pastas, *cantucci* cookies, and biscotti lure passersby into this sizable grocery shop.

 E4 S 34 151 RICHMOND ST.
617-523-8743 WWW.SALUMERIAITALIANA.COM

MAP 2 BEACON HILL

ANTIQUES AT 80 CHARLES *VINTAGE AND ANTIQUES*

A first stop for antique flatware collectors, this shop has an equally impressive stash of crystal, porcelain, and other timeworn, yet well-preserved, home accent pieces.

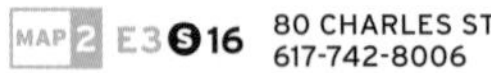
MAP 2 E3 S16 80 CHARLES ST.
617-742-8006

THE BEAUTY MARK *BATH, BEAUTY, AND SPA*

This indie answer to Sephora caters to connoisseurs of cult beauty products – among them Lola, Bumble & Bumble, Decleor, Venom, and Delux Beauty. Stationed on a postage stamp-size patch of Beacon Hill, it's a claustrophobe's worst nightmare and a narcissist's sweet dream.

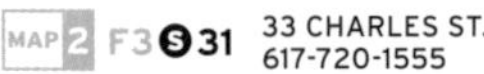
MAP 2 F3 S31 33 CHARLES ST.
617-720-1555

BLACK INK *GIFT AND HOME*

The trove of whimsical tchotchkes at this fun, funky store includes retro lunchboxes, bold wrapping papers, bullet-shaped cocktail shakers, and fleece dolls from Scary Stories.

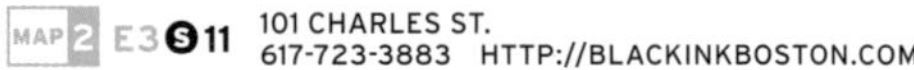
MAP 2 E3 S11 101 CHARLES ST.
617-723-3883 HTTP://BLACKINKBOSTON.COM

CHARLES STREET *SHOPPING DISTRICT*

This quaint, historic avenue is lined with a mix of tony, traditional antique shops, preppie boutiques, and hip entities, such as Good, Koo de Kir, and The Beauty Mark.

MAP 2 E3 S12 CHARLES ST. BTWN. BEACON AND CAMBRIDGE STS.
617-720-7888
WWW.BEACONHILLBUSINESSASSOCIATION.ORG

THE FLAT OF THE HILL *GIFT AND HOME*

The Flat of the Hill embodies Beacon Hill's Brahmin side. Pretty bottles of scented linen water, "Gone to Nantucket" message boards, and floral table settings are all in the spotlight.

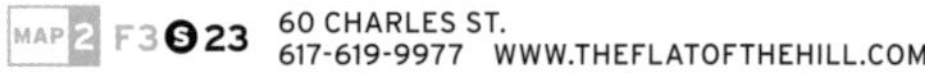
MAP 2 F3 S23 60 CHARLES ST.
617-619-9977 WWW.THEFLATOFTHEHILL.COM

FRENCH DRESSING *CLOTHING*

Beneath Boston's buttoned-up exterior lie lacy unmentionables from this jewel box of a lingerie shop. Provocative yet practical, the stock includes staples from Cosabella, Eberjey, Hanky Panky, Le Mystere, Skin, and Underglam.

MAP 2 F3 S25 49 RIVER ST.
617-723-4968 WWW.FRENCHDRESSINGLINGERIE.COM

HOLIDAY *CLOTHING AND SHOES*

Think Audrey Hepburn in *Charade* and you have the fashion philosophy of Holiday, where local heroines rifle the racks for cocktail dresses and cult couture. Well-bred and winsome, the look includes labels like Mint, Tracey Reese, and Rock & Republic.

MAP 2 F3 S24 53 CHARLES ST.
617-973-9730

SHOPS

BLACK INK

SAVENOR'S MARKET

KOO DE KIR *GIFT AND HOME*

A wonderland for *Wallpaper* subscribers, this store's housewares range from agate coasters to reversible tables. Catering to fashionistas is an intriguing selection of upscale accessories and designer jewelry.

 F3 Ⓢ32 65 CHESTNUT ST.
617-723-8111 WWW.KOODEKIR.COM

MOXIE *SHOES*

You don't have to be Imelda Marcos to max out your Visa at this small but selective shoe store. Taking patrons from clambakes to charity balls are seasonal styles by Cynthia Rowley, L'Autre Chose, Isaac, and Rafe.

 F3 Ⓢ26 51 CHARLES ST.
617-557-9991 HTTP://MOXIEBOSTON.COM

ROOM WITH A VIEUX ANTIQUES *VINTAGE AND ANTIQUES*

Plenty of French and English lovelies – marble-topped dressers, delicate mahogany armoires, elegant and unique accessories – are featured in this well-kept shop.

MAP 2 F3 Ⓢ35 20 CHARLES ST.
617-973-6600

SAVENOR'S MARKET *GOURMET GOODIES*

Known for its cases filled with unusual meats (zebra or buffalo, anyone?), Savenor's, a family establishment for two generations, also does well with fresh produce, artisanal cheese, and imported sweets and snacks.

 D4 Ⓢ5 160 CHARLES ST.
617-723-6328 WWW.SAVENORSMARKET.COM

UPSTAIRS DOWNSTAIRS ANTIQUES *VINTAGE AND ANTIQUES*

Unexpected finds are the norm in this hidden maze of old carpets, silverware, and cut glass. Tucked away in other cases are bounties of another sort: timeworn coins, antique dolls, old magazines, and ancient mirrors.

 E3 Ⓢ13 93 CHARLES ST.
617-367-1950

WISH *CLOTHING*

If you pine for adorable design on the girly side, Beacon Hill's Wish is at your command. Upgrade your wardrobe with lounge-worthy workout togs and frilly frocks by the likes of Tibi, Milly, and Nanette Lapore.

MAP 2 F3 S 28 49 CHARLES ST.
617-227-4441 WWW.WISHSTYLE.COM

MAP 3 DOWNTOWN/CHINATOWN

ARI BOSTON *CLOTHING AND SHOES*

This small boutique for the well-heeled man offers finely made casual wear downstairs and custom-tailored suits upstairs. A selection of ties in both classic and clever patterns punctuates the selection.

 A5 S 11 6 LIBERTY SQUARE
617-742-2202

BRATTLE BOOKSHOP *BOOKS AND MUSIC*

Bibliophiles break into a cold sweat when confronted with the titles at this three-story space, which is one of the oldest antiquarian bookshops in America. Its crowded shelves stock everything from vintage *Life* magazines (find one from your birth date) to first editions by Fitzgerald and Hemingway.

 B3 S 28 9 WEST ST.
617-542-0210 WWW.BRATTLEBOOKSHOP.COM

DOWNTOWN CROSSING *SHOPPING DISTRICT AND CENTER*

With the original (and best) Filene's Basement location and H&M in its stable, Downtown Crossing has a wrap on much of Boston's bargain shopping. Macy's, Skechers, and others round out the selection.

 B3 S 33 WASHINGTON ST. BTWN. WINTER AND STUART STS.
617-482-2139 WWW.DOWNTOWNCROSSING.ORG

EXHALE MIND/BODY SPA *BATH, BEAUTY, AND SPA*

Beauty isn't just skin-deep at this holistic oasis, where you can pamper your body with innovative spa treatments while expanding your mind with yoga, acupuncture, and "Core Fusion" classes.

 B1 S 17 28 ARLINGTON ST., AT THE HERITAGE ON THE GARDEN
617-532-7000 WWW.EXHALESPA.COM

FILENE'S BASEMENT *CLOTHING AND SHOES*

Filene's is the mother of all bargain bunkers. Each week sees new arrivals of high-end designer clothes for men, women, and children (plus accessories and home goods), which intrepid shoppers seize upon with an adrenaline rush.

 B3 S 29 426 WASHINGTON ST.
617-426-6645 WWW.FILENESBASEMENT.COM

VESSEL *GIFT AND HOME*

What started as a workshop for "candelas" (wireless rechargeable lamps) is now a forum for innovative housewares and accessories – among them worktables with storage space, fusionware china, and "tempo tags," clip-on digital watches that can be worn as hairpins or cuff links.

MAP 3 C3 S 50 125 KINGSTON ST.
617-292-0982 WWW.VESSEL.COM

DOWNTOWN CROSSING VESSEL

VINH KAN GINSENG CO. *GOURMET GOODIES*
With shelves lined with fresh noodles, eight different kinds of fish sauce, bean paste, and lychee gummy candies, Vinh Kan will fulfill almost any Asian ingredient need.

C2 Ⓢ44 675 WASHINGTON ST.
617-338-9028

ZAREH INC. *CLOTHING AND SHOES*
A trip to this downtown boutique will refine any man's wardrobe. Unique cuff links, custom-made suits, tailored pants, and button-downs all lend style with substance.

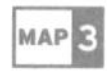

B5 Ⓢ36 1 LIBERTY SQUARE
617-350-6070

MAP 4 BACK BAY/SOUTH END

THE ANDOVER SHOP *CLOTHING AND SHOES*
You can take the man out of the boarding school, but you can't take the boarding school out of the man's wardrobe. When only Shetland wool, Scottish tweed, patch madras, and classic khaki will do, proper Bostonians beat a path to the Andover Shop.

B5 Ⓢ22 234 CLARENDON ST.
617-247-3344 WWW.THEANDOVERSHOP.COM

BARNEYS NEW YORK *CLOTHING AND SHOES*
Toto, we're not in Boston anymore . . . or are we? From the Italian chandelier in the Lanvin section to the working fireplace in the shoe salon, the New York department store has brought Madison Avenue glitz to the Back Bay.

C4 Ⓢ48 COPLEY PLACE MALL, 100 HUNTINGTON AVE.
617-385-3300 WWW.BARNEYS.COM

BLISS HOME *GIFT AND HOME*
Owner Panamai Manadee scours the globe to stock Bliss with both classic and cool home accessories. Costa Boda glassware, eel-skin-covered dressers, and brightly colored '60s-era ceramics are some of the highlights.

B5 Ⓢ21 121 NEWBURY ST.
617-421-5544 WWW.BLISSHOME.COM

BONPOINT *KIDS STUFF*

Children's wear this may be, but play clothes it is not. When the tykes need a little luxury, bring them here for beautifully made jumpers, dresses, or sport coats.

MAP 4 B6 Ⓢ 34 18 ARLINGTON ST.
617-267-1717 WWW.BONPOINT.COM

BRIX *GOURMET GOODIES*

You'll find the foundations for a great cellar at this atmospheric wine and spirits boutique, where underlit shelves draw the eye to featured bottles. Stop in for a weekend wine tasting, when they break out the crystal stemware and share the latest vintages.

MAP 4 F6 Ⓢ 80 1284 WASHINGTON ST.
617-542-2749 WWW.BRIXWINESHOP.COM

THE CLOSET *VINTAGE AND ANTIQUES*

The Closet avoids the disarray characteristic of vintage shops with its neat racks of gently used designer clothes from labels like Gucci, Ann Demeulemeester, and Isaac Mizrahi.

MAP 4 B4 Ⓢ 18 175 NEWBURY ST.
617-536-1919

COPLEY PLACE *SHOPPING CENTER*

The city's high-end mall of choice, Copley Place attracts the well-to-do with such stand-alone boutiques as Gucci, Louis Vuitton, Coach, Tiffany & Co., Montblanc, and Boston's first full-scale Barneys.

MAP 4 C4 Ⓢ 49 100 HUNTINGTON AVE.
617-369-5000 WWW.SIMON.COM

DORFMAN *ACCESSORIES AND JEWELRY*

This small, old-world store purveys classic pieces, like ruby chokers and diamond drop earrings, with personal service to match.

MAP 4 B6 Ⓢ 31 24 NEWBURY ST.
617-536-2022

ERMENEGILDO ZEGNA *CLOTHING AND SHOES*

The crème de la crème of men's suiting is found right here, where sumptuous silk shirts, light-as-a-feather linen trousers, and refined cotton suits hang primly. Some casual pieces – equally well made – are downstairs.

MAP 4 B6 Ⓢ 26 39 NEWBURY ST.
617-424-9300 WWW.ZEGNA.COM

GARAGE SALE *GIFT AND HOME*

Flea markets don't get any more fabulous than this outpost for high-end consignments, which benefits from the eclectic tastes of its South End neighborhood. Outfit your home with upscale resale you could never afford new – from crystal chandeliers to bergère chairs.

MAP 4 E5 Ⓢ 75 55 WALTHAM ST.
617-482-7044

G SPA *BATH, BEAUTY, AND SPA*

Sick of the Enya you hear over the average spa speakers? At G Spa, "splurge" facials can be paired with a personally programmed

METROSEXUAL MILE

It may be set in New York, but *Queer Eye for the Straight Guy* got its start in Boston's own South End. And you'll see why when you hit the metrosexual mile of Tremont Street, where you'll find the materials for your own makeover on the racks at urban chic **Uniform** (511 Tremont St., 617-247-2360, www.uniformboston.com). The South End isn't the only neighborhood where it's raining menswear, as evidenced by the bumper crop of shops like **Market (p. 51)** on Newbury Street, **Modo Gatto (p. 45)** in the North End and upscale **Ari Boston (p. 48)** in the Financial District. And if you thought spa treatments and testosterone were mutually exclusive, **Exhale Mind/Body Spa (p. 48)** will change your mind with its man-friendly Metro Facial.

iPod. Those with less time to indulge can opt for a "quickie" – a short but intense program of pampering for the face, hands, feet, body, or hair.

 **27** 35 NEWBURY ST. 617-267-4772 WWW.GSPA.BIZ

JASMINE SOLA *CLOTHING AND SHOES*

Mixing fashionable designs with feminine cuts, this small chain boutique carries frilly cocktail dresses, swaggering silk pants, and complementary jewelry and accessories.

 **6** 344 NEWBURY ST. 617-867-4636 WWW.JASMINESOLA.COM

LOUIS BOSTON *CLOTHING AND SHOES*

What Barneys is to New York, Louis is to Boston: an index for the ultimate in modern design. While metrosexual men gravitate to labels like Dries Van Noten and Blue Blood, female fashionistas swoon over the latest from Prada, Zac Posen, and Tuleh.

 **29** 234 BERKELEY ST. 617-262-6100 WWW.LOUISBOSTON.COM

MARKET *CLOTHING AND SHOES*

To Market, to Market, to find a new style, the most man-friendly shop on the Newbury mile. Proving that taste and testosterone are not mutually exclusive, this haven for metrosexual menswear stocks Theory, Gaultier, Cavalli, and other European designers.

 **20** 141 NEWBURY ST. 617-425-0006 WWW.MARKETFASHION.COM

MATSU *CLOTHING AND SHOES*

Sequined, feathery numbers by Rozae Nichols flank silk tunics by Comme des Garçons in this artfully presented shop, where owner

NEWBURY STREET

VELLUM

Dava Muramatsu showcases the edgy-but-tasteful pieces she culls from all over the globe.

 259 NEWBURY ST.
617-266-9707 WWW.MATSUBOSTON.COM

MICHAUD COSMEDIX *BATH, BEAUTY, AND SPA*
Julie Michaud is known as the city's arch angel: She shapes the best brows in town. She and her team also do makeup, micropigmentation (also known as cosmetic tattooing), and eyelash extensions.

 69 NEWBURY ST., 5TH FL.
617-262-1607 WWW.MICHAUDCOSMEDIX.COM

NEWBURY STREET *SHOPPING DISTRICT*
Boston's answer to the Champs-Élysées, this *rue* is packed with unique shops and tony chains alike. Chanel, Vera Wang, Marc Jacobs – if it's hip, high-end, or happening, you'll find it here.

 NEWBURY ST. BTWN. ARLINGTON ST. AND MASSACHUSETTS AVE.
617-267-2224 WWW.NEWBURYSTREETLEAGUE.ORG

9 MONTHS *CLOTHING AND SHOES*
There's always bugaboo gridlock at this stylish store, which was founded on the premise that maternity shouldn't have to mean taking leave of your fashion sense. With designs by NOM, Japanese Weekend, and Olian, you'll wish your due date would never come.

 286 NEWBURY ST.
617-236-5523 WWW.9MONTHSINC.COM

PARLOR *CLOTHING AND SHOES*
Your boyfriend can boot up in the wireless lounge while you sample kicky skirts, after-dark dresses, and other cool clothing from the likes of Free People, Nicholas K., and Porridge. Be sure to check the sale bins, where last season's styles can be found at up to 70 percent off.

 1248 WASHINGTON ST.
617-521-9005

PRUDENTIAL CENTER
See SIGHTS, p. 10.

 800 BOYLSTON ST.
617-236-3100 WWW.PRUDENTIALCENTER.COM

QUEEN BEE *CLOTHING AND SHOES*

Pink and green is spoken here, where you'll find fresh spins on preppie staples like seersucker shorts, madras sundresses, striped ribbon belts, and canvas espadrilles. Formerly Eye of the Needle, Queen Bee stocks Milly, Shoshanna, Diane Von Furstenberg, and others.

 B5 ⓢ23 85 NEWBURY ST.
617-859-7999 WWW.QUEENBEEGIRLS.COM

SHREVE, CRUMP & LOW *ACCESSORIES AND JEWELRY*

A two-story Steuben glass installation serves as the centerpiece of this jeweler's new space, where classic lines mingle with mod designs by Gucci, Vera Wang, and Seaman Schepps. It's a first stop for Brahmin brides in search of extravagant engagement rings, divine china, and gorgeous glassware.

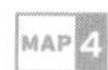 C6 ⓢ57 440 BOYLSTON ST.
617-267-9100 WWW.SHREVECRUMPANDLOW.COM

TRIDENT BOOKSELLERS & CAFÉ *BOOKS AND MUSIC*

A bohemian oasis on commercial Newbury Street, Trident has a comprehensive selection of new books and obscure periodicals – all of them available for browsing over a mocha latte or grilled cheese on challah.

 B2 ⓢ7 338 NEWBURY ST.
617-267-8688 WWW.TRIDENTBOOKSCAFE.COM

VELLUM *GIFT AND HOME*

Correspondence is an art form with exquisite stationery from Vellum, where the paper is so nice you'll want to use it twice. Journals, pens, ink, and albums are available, along with the world's most gorgeous gift wrap.

 D4 ⓢ63 55 DARTMOUTH ST.
617-247-2323 WWW.VELLUMSTORE.COM

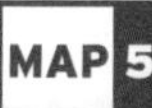

FENWAY/KENMORE SQUARE

COMMONWEALTH BOOKS *BOOKS AND MUSIC*

This Kenmore Square outpost of the famous bookstore caters to casual browsers and serious collectors alike, stocking its towering shelves with scholarly, used, antiquarian, and out-of-print titles.

 C5 ⓢ9 526 COMMONWEALTH AVE.
617-236-0182 WWW.COMMONWEALTHBOOKS.COM

FANNY AND DELPHINE *CLOTHING AND SHOES*

Accessible, artsy styles are the signature of this women's boutique, where New England salvage serves as the setting for contemporary couture from Japan, Italy, France, and Scandinavia. A little slice of Newbury Street in Kenmore Square.

 C5 ⓢ11 522 COMMONWEALTH AVE.
617-266-2006 WWW.FANNYANDDELPHINE.COM

PREPPIE CHIC BOUTIQUES

Gone are the days when Boston's fashion identity was defined by headbands and khakis, but there will always be a place for preppies here. Elbow patches are all the rage at Porter Square's **Keezer's (p. 58),** a shrine for the tweed-inclined that specializes in the gently used cast-offs of Harvard students. Partisans of pink and green beat a path to Newbury Street's **Queen Bee (p. 53),** where the racks are rife with ribbon belts, madras shorts, and seersucker sundresses. And just around the corner on Clarendon lies **The Andover Shop (p. 49),** a haven for conservative couture that takes its name from the elite boarding school.

JEAN THERAPY *CLOTHING AND SHOES*

Whatever your jeans neurosis, the answer is in stock at this Kenmore Square denim depot. All the hottest, most hype-worthy styles – and personalized service – will guide you to the perfect pair.

MAP 5 C5 S 10 HOTEL COMMONWEALTH, 524 COMMONWEALTH AVE.
617-266-6555 WWW.JEAN-THERAPY.COM

NANTUCKET NATURAL OILS *BATH, BEAUTY, AND SPA*

Madonna and Aerosmith's Steven Tyler are among the devotees of this specialty fragrance bar, which crafts intoxicating original scents and alcohol-free versions of designer perfumes and colognes.

MAP 5 C5 S 13 HOTEL COMMONWEALTH, 508 COMMONWEALTH AVE.
617-437-9800 WWW.NANTUCKETNATURALOILS.COM

PANOPTICON GALLERY OF PHOTOGRAPHY *GIFT AND HOME*

Train your eye on images from emerging and established artists, or examine archival reproductions of works by Bradford Washburn, Ernest C. Withers, Vittorio Sella, and others.

MAP 5 C5 S 15 HOTEL COMMONWEALTH, 502C COMMONWEALTH AVE.
617-267-8929 WWW.PANOPT.COM

PERSONA *ACCESSORIES AND JEWELRY*

The emphasis is on individual style at this eclectic jewelry shop, which also stocks cashmere swaddling blankets, hand-printed stationery, and other upscale indulgences. Complimentary valet parking is available.

MAP 5 C5 S 14 HOTEL COMMONWEALTH, 504 COMMONWEALTH AVE.
617-266-3003 WWW.PERSONASTYLE.COM

THE SOUVENIR STORE *CLOTHING AND SHOES*

Conveniently located within bunting distance of the Fenway, this comprehensive shop is the next best thing to raiding the Red Sox locker room, offering everything from bobbleheads to Big Papi jerseys.

MAP 5 D4 S 21 19 YAWKEY WAY
617-421-8686 WWW.YAWKEYWAYSTORE.COM

STUDIO FOR HAIR *BATH, BEAUTY, AND SPA*

Painter Anthony Vitale co-owns this salon and infuses it with the same aplomb he brings to the canvas. A miracle worker for corrective coloring emergencies, he also gets it right the first time.

MAP 5 C5 S 19 464 COMMONWEALTH AVE.
617-262-2029

TEMPER CHOCOLATES *GOURMET GOODIES*

As the former pastry chef at Manhattan's Gotham Grill, Caroline Yeh knows from chocolate. And what she knows is now available in bon bon form at Boston's hottest sweets boutique. Endanger your teeth with bite-sized bliss, infused with flavors ranging from Madagascan ganache to single malt scotch.

MAP 5 C5 S 17 HOTEL COMMONWEALTH, 500 COMMONWEALTH AVE.
617-375-2255 WWW.TEMPERCHOCOLATES.COM

WINE GALLERY *GOURMET GOODIES*

The name says it all: These wines weren't just picked at random, they were curated with a connoisseur's attention to excellence. In addition to European and New World vintages, the shop has an encyclopedic selection of domestic, imported, and artisanal beers.

MAP 5 C5 S 12 HOTEL COMMONWEALTH, 516 COMMONWEALTH AVE.
617-266-9300 WWW.WINE-GALLERY.COM

MAP 6 CAMBRIDGE/HARVARD SQUARE

ALPHA OMEGA *ACCESSORIES AND JEWELRY*

When it comes to wedding rings and high-end bling, the selection at Alpha Omega is as ambitious as its name suggests. Chat with an in-house diamond specialist or browse baubles from the likes of Bulgari, Vacheron Constantin, Simon G., and Kirk Kara.

MAP 6 D3 S 34 1380 MASSACHUSETTS AVE.
617-864-1227 WWW.ALPHAOMEGAJEWELERS.COM

BEAUTY AND MAIN *BATH, BEAUTY, AND SPA*

When Maybelline just won't do, beauty addicts beat a path to Beauty and Main, where cult cosmetics are the name of the game. The growing chain is smaller and more selective than Sephora, stocking skincare, fragrances, and makeup by names like Laura Mercier, Bliss, Darphin, Fresh, and Creed.

MAP 6 D3 S 22 30 BRATTLE ST.
617-868-7171 WWW.BEAUTYANDMAIN.COM

CARDULLO'S *GOURMET GOODIES*

Entering this mecca of international foods on an empty stomach can be a downright dangerous thing, with rotund breads, delectable chocolates, and tangy jams tempting you from all sides.

MAP 6 D3 S 29 6 BRATTLE ST.
617-491-8888 WWW.CARDULLOS.COM

COMMA *BATH, BEAUTY, AND SPA*

Say *sayonara* to stress with services ranging from shiatsu to fire cupping. Specializing in Japanese massage techniques, this Harvard Square oasis also offers reiki, *sotai ho, gua sha,* and moxibustion.

MAP 6 D2 S 12 127 MT. AUBURN ST.
617-547-2700 WWW.COMMA-INC.COM

CURIOUS GEORGE GOES TO WORDSWORTH *KIDS STUFF*

Engage the attention span of your own mischievous monkey with a visit to this Harvard Square institution, where plush toys and board games share the shelves with titles from *Babar* to Lemony Snicket.

MAP 6 D3 S 30 1 JOHN F. KENNEDY ST.
617-498-0062 WWW.CURIOUSG.COM

GROLIER POETRY BOOK SHOP *BOOKS AND MUSIC*

Founded in 1927, Harvard Square's postage stamp-size store is the country's oldest freestanding bookshop entirely devoted to poetry. Verse from all time periods and cultures has a place on the shelves.

MAP 6 E4 S 46 6 PLYMPTON ST.
617-547-4648 WWW.GROLIERPOETRYBOOKSHOP.COM

HARVARD BOOK STORE *BOOKS AND MUSIC*

Academia and pop culture merge here, blending and mingling among shelves of new (upstairs) and used (downstairs) books.

MAP 6 E4 S 47 1256 MASSACHUSETTS AVE.
617-661-1515 WWW.HARVARD.COM

THE HARVARD COOP *BOOKS AND MUSIC*

Arguably the true anchor of Harvard Square, the Coop started in 1882 as a nonprofit Harvard enterprise. These days it's decidedly more commercial: Owned by Barnes & Noble, it sells stacks of discounted books and many souvenirs emblazoned with the Harvard emblem.

MAP 6 D3 S 33 1400 MASSACHUSETTS AVE.
617-499-2000 WWW.HARVARD.BKSTORE.COM

HARVARD SQUARE *SHOPPING DISTRICT*

The bohemian Harvard Square of yesterday still lingers along the redbrick sidewalks in local bookstores, cafés, boutiques, and gourmet grocers.

MAP 6 D3 S 28 INTERSECTION OF MASSACHUSETTS AVE., BRATTLE AND JOHN F. KENNEDY STS.;
617-491-3434
WWW.HARVARDSQUARE.COM

J. PRESS *CLOTHING AND SHOES*

The epitome of Ivy League dress sits just outside Harvard. If it's traditional prep-wear for men, it's here: mallard-dotted belts, khakis, button-down Oxford shirts, and yes, penny loafers.

MAP 6 E3 S 42 82 MT. AUBURN ST.
617-547-9886 WWW.JPRESSONLINE.COM

L. A. BURDICK CHOCOLATE *GOURMET GOODIES*

The most refined chocolates around – tiny dark truffles, milk chocolate cranberry pieces, and ganache squares – are under

L. A. BURDICK CHOCOLATE

MINT JULEP

Burdick's glass cases. Don't miss the adorably delicious mouse- and penguin-shaped truffles.

MAP 6 C2 S 6 52D BRATTLE ST.
617-491-4340 WWW.BURDICKCHOCOLATE.COM

MINT JULEP *CLOTHING AND SHOES*

As refreshing as the drink for which it's named, this bountiful boutique brings a welcome splash of originality to chain-choked Harvard Square. Here you'll find fab handbags, eye-catching accessories, and flattering, fun fashions from Ella Moss, Tibi, Lulu Guinness, and other offbeat designers.

MAP 6 D3 S 23 6 CHURCH ST.
617-576-6468 WWW.SHOPMINTJULEP.COM

MUSEUM OF USEFUL THINGS *GIFT AND HOME*

This clever home shop has everything you need to give your pad some character. Pick up retro aluminum house numbers, a cartoon-shaped bath mat, or the world's most stylish humane mousetrap.

MAP 6 C3 S 8 49B BRATTLE ST.
617-576-3322 WWW.THEMUT.COM

NEWBURY COMICS *BOOKS AND MUSIC*

More than a comics shack, this is the alternative listener's shop of choice. Look for a solid selection of rock, pop, and indie sounds, plus racks of magazines and gifts – some cute, some tacky, and some cheeky.

MAP 6 D3 S 32 36 JOHN F. KENNEDY ST.
617-491-0337 WWW.NEWBURYCOMICS.COM

OONA'S *VINTAGE AND ANTIQUES*

There are plenty of finds for men and women on Oona's jumbled racks. Several rooms are full of retro fur coats, brightly printed dresses, sleek motorcycle jackets, and frilly hats and accessories.

MAP 6 E4 S 49 1210 MASSACHUSETTS AVE.
617-491-2654

THE TANNERY *CLOTHING AND SHOES*

It's not much to look at, but this subterranean shoe store has the most comprehensive selection in Harvard Square. More for everyday wear than evening elegance, the brands include Chinese Laundry, Ugg Australia, Mephisto, Lacoste, and Palladium.

MAP 6 D3 S 24 11A BRATTLE ST. 617-491-0810 WWW.THETANNERY.COM

TEALUXE *GOURMET GOODIES*

A city favorite, Tealuxe is the place to pick up any of the hundreds of exotic international blends for later enjoyment or a spice-laced chai latte for instant gratification.

MAP 6 D3 S 25 0 BRATTLE ST. 617-441-0077 WWW.TEALUXE.COM

OVERVIEW MAP

KEEZER'S *CLOTHING AND SHOES*

Who cares what the diploma says – anyone can look like an Ivy Leaguer with a trip to this extravagantly stocked used clothing shop, where the wares come from the closets of tweedy Harvard alums.

OVERVIEW MAP **C2** 140 RIVER ST. 617-547-2455 WWW.KEEZERS.COM

ARTS AND LEISURE

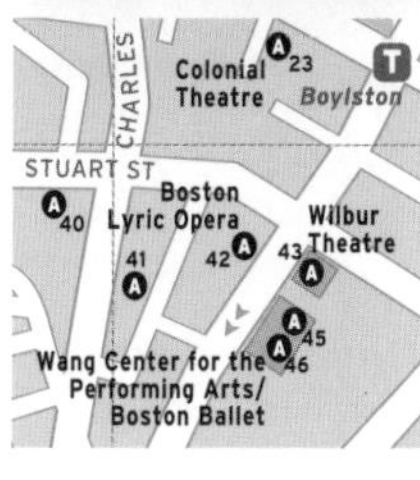

Best place to experience the heritage of the American Revolution: **OLD SOUTH MEETING HOUSE,** p. 62

Best place to see fossils: **PEABODY MUSEUM OF ARCHAEOLOGY AND ETHNOLOGY,** p. 65

Best place for cutting-edge art: **INSTITUTE OF CONTEMPORARY ART,** p. 62

Best place to imagine life as a Boston Brahmin: **GIBSON HOUSE MUSEUM,** p. 63

Best Newbury Street gallery: **BARBARA KRAKOW GALLERY,** p. 62

Best place for new drama: **BOSTON CENTER FOR THE ARTS,** p. 70

Most thought-provoking theater: **AMERICAN REPERTORY THEATRE,** p. 71

Best place to see flicks from the past: **BRATTLE THEATRE,** p. 71

Best venue for live rock music: **ORPHEUM THEATRE,** p. 69

Best place for a laugh: **COMEDY CONNECTION,** p. 67

Best place to jog: **THE ESPLANADE,** p. 73

Prettiest spot for a walk: **PUBLIC GARDEN,** p. 7

Best ocean views: Ferry to **BOSTON HARBOR ISLANDS,** p. 73

Best in-city escape from the city: **ARNOLD ARBORETUM,** p. 76

Best place for a picnic: **CHRISTOPHER COLUMBUS PARK,** p. 73

MUSEUMS AND GALLERIES

MAP 1 NORTH END/GOVERNMENT CENTER

SPORTS MUSEUM

Memorabilia from Boston's professional sports teams reflect the region's die-hard loyalty to its beloved squads. Sections are dedicated to basketball, baseball, hockey, and football, as well as soccer and boxing.

MAP 1 C2 2 100 LEGENDS WAY, TD BANKNORTH GARDEN, 5TH AND 6TH FLS.
617-624-1234 WWW.SPORTSMUSEUM.ORG

USS *CONSTITUTION*

See SIGHTS, p. 3.

MAP 1 A5 1 CHARLESTOWN NAVY YARD
617-426-1812 WWW.USSCONSTITUTIONMUSEUM.ORG

MAP 2 BEACON HILL

BOSTON ATHENAEUM

This historic research library boasts stellar special collections that range from Lord Byron first editions to Confederacy state documents to Gypsy literature. The athenaeum is for members only, but the first floor, which has changing exhibits, is open to the public and tours are available.

MAP 2 F6 44 10 1/2 BEACON ST.
617-227-0270 WWW.BOSTONATHENAEUM.ORG

HARRISON GRAY OTIS HOUSE

Designed by Charles Bulfinch in 1796 for friend and one-time Boston mayor Harrison Gray Otis, this meticulously renovated Federalist-style home illuminates the way of life for the Boston elite in the post-Revolutionary War era.

MAP 2 E5 20 141 CAMBRIDGE ST.
617-227-3956
WWW.HISTORICNEWENGLAND.ORG/VISIT/HOMES/OTIS.HTM

MUSEUM OF AFRO-AMERICAN HISTORY

Set in the Abiel Smith School, which was built as an all-black institute in 1834, this museum traces the history and culture of African American Bostonians. Adjacent is the African Meeting House, the oldest black church in America.

MAP 2 E5 22 46 JOY ST.
617-725-0022 WWW.AFROAMMUSEUM.ORG

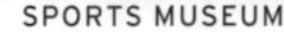

SPORTS MUSEUM BERNARD TOALE GALLERY

MUSEUM OF SCIENCE

Learn the latest keyboard magic in the Current Science & Technology Center or watch sparks fly in the Theater of Electricity. If you tire of the hard sciences, check the museum's hatching chicks or playful tamarind monkeys, or take a break in the exquisite butterfly garden.

 4

SCIENCE PARK ALONG RTE. 28
617-723-2500 WWW.MOS.ORG

NICHOLS HOUSE MUSEUM

The home (from 1885 to 1960) of writer and feminist Rose Standish Nichols, this Federalist-style townhouse reflects 19th- and early 20th-century life on Beacon Hill.

 38

55 MT. VERNON ST.
617-227-6993 WWW.NICHOLSHOUSEMUSEUM.ORG

MAP 3 DOWNTOWN/CHINATOWN

BERNARD TOALE GALLERY

Toale pioneered the art migration from gallery-heavy Newbury Street to the SoWa (south of Washington) area in 1998. His space displays contemporary works and also houses the Boston Drawing Project, designed to bring works on paper to a broader audience.

 61

450 HARRISON AVE.
617-482-2477 WWW.BERNARDTOALEGALLERY.COM

BOSTON CHILDREN'S MUSEUM

After a major expansion and renovation, the museum offers educational and purely fun exhibits geared for the toddler to 10-year-old crowd. The distinctive 40-foot milk bottle outside would hold 58,000 gallons of the white stuff.

MAP 3 D5 A 58

300 CONGRESS ST.
617-426-8855 WWW.BOSTONCHILDRENSMUSEUM.ORG

BOSTON TEA PARTY SHIPS & MUSEUM

Under renovation until 2008, reproductions of two of the three ships that held the ill-fated tea during the American Revolution let visitors relive history by tossing a bale of tea (attached by rope) over the side.

 C5 A 55

CONGRESS ST. BRIDGE
617-338-1773 WWW.BOSTONTEAPARTYSHIP.COM

INSTITUTE OF CONTEMPORARY ART

This now-major Boston institution recently relocated to a 65,000-square-foot building on the waterfront. Long a venue for exhibits of the new new thing, the museum continues to showcase multi-disciplinary contemporary arts.

MAP 3 D6 Ⓐ60 100 NORTHERN AVE.
617-266-5152 WWW.ICABOSTON.ORG

OLD SOUTH MEETING HOUSE

Built in 1729 as a Puritan meetinghouse, the Old South witnessed the birth of the American Revolution and countless social movements since then. It has remained a forum for fiery and/or controversial speech, as depicted in its permanent exhibit "Voices of Protest."

MAP 3 B4 Ⓐ35 310 WASHINGTON ST.
617-482-6439 WWW.OLDSOUTHMEETINGHOUSE.ORG

OLD STATE HOUSE MUSEUM

Built in 1713, the former state house is the oldest public building in Boston and today features displays on the city's culture and history. Just outside, a circle embedded in the pavement marks the location of the 1770 Boston Massacre.

MAP 3 A4 Ⓐ10 206 WASHINGTON ST.
617-720-1713 WWW.BOSTONHISTORY.ORG

MAP 4 BACK BAY/SOUTH END

BARBARA KRAKOW GALLERY

A veteran in Boston's contemporary art scene, Krakow shows multiple media – prints are the specialty – with a tendency toward minimalism. Chuck Close and Sol LeWitt are among the artists displayed here.

MAP 4 B6 Ⓐ33 10 NEWBURY ST., 5TH FL.
617-262-4490 WWW.BARBARAKRAKOWGALLERY.COM

BOSTON ARCHITECTURAL COLLEGE'S MCCORMICK GALLERY

This design and architectural college's gallery displays the work of students, neighborhood artists, and professionals. A trompe l'oeil decorates one side of the building.

MAP 4 B2 Ⓐ5 320 NEWBURY ST.
617-262-5000 WWW.THE-BAC.EDU

BOSTON PUBLIC LIBRARY

This 1895 granite building (a more modern wing was added in 1972) was the country's first publicly supported free municipal library. Check out the John Singer Sargent murals and stunning Bates reading room, or take a break in the soothing courtyard.

C4 Ⓐ43 700 BOYLSTON ST.
617-536-5400 WWW.BPL.ORG

BOSTON PUBLIC LIBRARY

GIBSON HOUSE MUSEUM

GIBSON HOUSE MUSEUM

In the 1930s, when wealthy eccentric Charles Hammond Gibson realized the Victorian era of his youth was vanishing, he decided to preserve everything – from the furniture to the wallpaper – in his 1860-built Back Bay mansion. The resulting museum is a peek into the nuances of a long-gone way of life.

MAP 4 A6 A1 137 BEACON ST.
617-267-6338 WWW.THEGIBSONHOUSE.ORG

HOWARD YEZERSKI GALLERY

One of the few Newbury Street galleries to promote new media, such as computer-generated prints and videos, the Howard Yezerski Gallery often goes straight for the abstract.

MAP 4 B6 A32 14 NEWBURY ST., 3RD FL.
617-262-0550 WWW.HOWARDYEZERSKIGALLERY.COM

PUCKER GALLERY

Ceramics from Japan and Korea and pottery masters like Brother Thomas and Phil Rogers are showcased here alongside paintings and sculptures in this intimate gallery, which also has Inuit and African art.

MAP 4 B4 A14 171 NEWBURY ST.
617-267-9473 WWW.PUCKERGALLERY.COM

ROBERT KLEIN GALLERY

World-class photo collector Robert Klein has more than 3,000 works in his must-see inventory, including shots by Ansel Adams, Man Ray, and Herb Ritts.

MAP 4 B6 A30 38 NEWBURY ST., 4TH FL.
617-267-7997 WWW.ROBERTKLEINGALLERY.COM

VOSE GALLERIES

Established in 1841, Vose is the great-granddaddy of Boston exhibition spaces and the oldest family-run gallery in the country. Specializing in high-end 18th-, 19th-, and early 20th-century artists, it also has a contemporary wing.

MAP 4 B3 A13 238 NEWBURY ST.
617-536-6176 WWW.VOSEGALLERIES.COM

MAP 5 FENWAY/KENMORE SQUARE

ISABELLA STEWART GARDNER MUSEUM

See SIGHTS, p. 13.

MAP 5 F3 34 280 THE FENWAY
617-566-1401 WWW.GARDNERMUSEUM.ORG

MUSEUM OF FINE ARTS

See SIGHTS, p. 14.

MAP 5 F4 37 465 HUNTINGTON AVE.
617-267-9300 WWW.MFA.ORG

SCHOOL OF THE MUSEUM OF FINE ARTS

The art school's name helps draw internationally known artists to its Grossman Gallery. Also check out what the students are up to – it could be the next big thing.

MAP 5 F4 36 230 THE FENWAY
617-267-6100 WWW.SMFA.EDU

MAP 6 CAMBRIDGE/HARVARD SQUARE

HARVARD MUSEUM OF NATURAL HISTORY

While the mesmerizing permanent display of 3,000 blown-glass botanical replicas – the famous "Glass Flowers" – remains the museum's main attraction, the zoological, mineralogical, and geological exhibits are worth an afternoon of exploration.

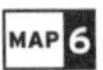
MAP 6 B5 4 HARVARD UNIVERSITY, 26 OXFORD ST.
617-495-3045 WWW.HMNH.HARVARD.EDU

HARVARD UNIVERSITY ART MUSEUMS

Harvard University has three major art museums, each with a distinct mission. The Fogg Art Museum has significant Renaissance and pre-Renaissance work, the Busch-Reisinger Museum has a collection of Germanic art of North and Central Europe, and the Arthur M. Sackler Museum focuses on ancient Asian and Islamic art. Beginning in summer 2008, the Fogg will be closed for renovation; important pieces will be moved to the Sackler and to a new Allston location.

MAP 6 D5 36 HARVARD UNIVERSITY, 32 QUINCY ST.
617-495-9400 WWW.ARTMUSEUMS.HARVARD.EDU

HURST GALLERY

Works and antiquities from Africa, the Pacific Islands, the Americas, and Asia are on display, as well as such special exhibits as "Indonesian Masks" and "Faces of the Buddha."

MAP 6 E3 44 53 MT. AUBURN ST. (DOOR ON PLIMPTON ST.)
617-491-6888 WWW.HURSTGALLERY.COM

LONGFELLOW NATIONAL HISTORIC SITE

Once George Washington's headquarters for part of the Revolutionary War, and later home to Henry Wadsworth Longfellow,

MUSEUM OF FINE ARTS

LONGFELLOW NATIONAL HISTORIC SITE

this space contains an extensive decorative arts collection, a 10,000-volume library, and Longfellow's photos and writings.

MAP 6 B1 Ⓐ 2 105 BRATTLE ST.
617-876-4491 WWW.NPS.GOV/LONG

PEABODY MUSEUM OF ARCHAEOLOGY AND ETHNOLOGY

One of the country's original anthropological museums, the Peabody has notable Mesoamerican offerings, including a Mayan temple staircase and pre-Colombian pottery. An exuberant Day of the Dead exhibit blends Mexican tradition with modern crafts.

MAP 6 C5 Ⓐ 10 HARVARD UNIVERSITY, 11 DIVINITY AVE.
617-496-1027 WWW.PEABODY.HARVARD.EDU

SEMITIC MUSEUM OF HARVARD UNIVERSITY

A meticulously created replica of an Iron Age home – complete with authentic artifacts – dominates the first floor of this small gem of a museum, which has significant displays of Egyptian and Middle East antiquities.

MAP 6 C6 Ⓐ 11 HARVARD UNIVERSITY, 6 DIVINITY AVE.
617-495-4631 WWW.FAS.HARVARD.EDU/~SEMITIC

OVERVIEW MAP

HAMILL GALLERY OF AFRICAN ART

Nearly 75 tribes are represented in this collection of close to 20,000 traditional African art pieces. The themed exhibits change every three months, and displayed items may include masks, figures, artifacts, textiles, jewelry, books, and posters.

OVERVIEW MAP **E3** 2164 WASHINGTON ST.
617-442-8204 WWW.HAMILLGALLERY.COM

JOHN F. KENNEDY NATIONAL HISTORIC SITE

JFK's birthplace and childhood home, purchased back by the Kennedys after his assassination, has been preserved as a historic site. It is open for tours from May 17 through September.

OVERVIEW MAP **D1** BROOKLINE, 83 BEALS ST.
617-566-7937 WWW.NPS.GOV/JOFI

MUSEUMS FARTHER AFIELD

With so many large world-class museums in Boston, it's often easy to forget that there are a number of world-class, if small-scale, institutions just outside the city. In the historic town of Lexington, the birth of the American revolution is well served by the **National Heritage Museum** (33 Marrett Rd., Lexington, 781-861-6559, www.nationalheritagemuseum.org). North of Boston in Salem, the expanded **Peabody Essex Museum** (East India Square, Salem, 978-745-9500, www.pem.org) explores New England's sailing history with outstanding collections of maritime, East India, and Far East artifacts including an entire historic Chinese house. The 35-acre grounds of the **DeCordova Museum and Sculpture Park** (51 Sandy Pond Rd., Lincoln, 781-259-8355, www.decordova.org) is dotted with nearly 80 outdoor sculptures, and inside, the museum has exhibits of contemporary art with an emphasis on up-and-coming artists.

LIST VISUAL ARTS CENTER

Housed in an I. M. Pei-designed building, MIT's primary art gallery, which features mixed-media contemporary art, aims to push beyond traditional concepts about art.

OVERVIEW MAP **C3** CAMBRIDGE, MIT, 20 AMES ST., BLDG. E15, ATRIUM LEVEL
617-253-4680 HTTP://WEB.MIT.EDU/LVAC

MIT MUSEUM

With exhibits that range from holograms and kinetic sculptures to artificial intelligence and Kismet, the first sociable robot, the museum will make visitors wonder: "Is this science or art? Or both?"

OVERVIEW MAP **C3** CAMBRIDGE, MIT, 265 MASSACHUSETTS AVE.
617-253-4444
WEB.MIT.EDU/MUSEUM

OFF MAP

JOHN F. KENNEDY PRESIDENTIAL LIBRARY AND MUSEUM

See SIGHTS, p. 16.

OFF MAP COLUMBIA POINT
866-535-1960 WWW.JFKLIBRARY.ORG

PERFORMING ARTS

MAP 1 NORTH END/GOVERNMENT CENTER

COMEDY CONNECTION *COMEDY*

Housed in Faneuil Hall, the city's oldest comedy club draws national acts such as Anthony Clark, Jon Stewart, and David Brenner on weekends and features the best of local talent during the week.

 F4 46 245 QUINCY MARKET PLACE, 2ND FL.
617-248-9700 WWW.COMEDYCONNECTIONBOSTON.COM

IMPROV ASYLUM *COMEDY*

Audience participation is welcome during these improvisations and sketch comedies. Nothing fazes the comic team – yell out "Chilean sea bass" or "lederhosen," and the troupe will seamlessly work it into their schtick.

 E4 31 216 HANOVER ST.
617-263-6887 WWW.IMPROVASYLUM.COM

KING'S CHAPEL MUSIC *CONCERTS*

A lengthy musical heritage – it was New England's first church to get an organ in 1713 – continues with free lunch-hour recitals Tuesdays and a Sunday series featuring groups such as the Handel & Haydn Society.

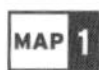 F2 41 58 TREMONT ST.
617-227-2155 WWW.KINGS-CHAPEL.ORG

BOSTIX

To score tickets at reduced rates, visit one of the two BosTix kiosks – one outside Faneuil Hall, the other in Copley Square – where you can buy half-price tickets (cash only) the day of the show. Get to the location by 9:30 A.M. (it opens at 10 A.M.) on Friday, Saturday, and Sunday for the best seats. The BosTix booths also have information on events around Boston and sell full-price tickets via Ticketmaster. The service is run by ArtsBoston (617-262-8532, www.artsboston.org), a nonprofit group representing 160 Greater Boston arts organizations.

MAP 2 BEACON HILL

HATCH SHELL *VARIOUS*

Most known for the always-mobbed July Fourth Boston Pops concert, the amphitheater on the bank of the Charles River features other events, such as the daylong Earthfest music festival, Boston Blues Festival, and Free Friday Flicks, classic films shown at sunset.

  THE ESPLANADE
617-727-1300 WWW.MASS.GOV/DCR/HATCH_EVENTS.HTM

MAP 3 DOWNTOWN/CHINATOWN

BOSTON BALLET *DANCE*

The first repertory ballet in New England when founded in 1963, this company stays true to such classics as *Swan Lake* and *The Sleeping Beauty* and is routinely ranked among the top in the country.

 C2 Ⓐ45 WANG THEATRE, 270 TREMONT ST.
617-695-6950 WWW.BOSTONBALLET.ORG

BOSTON LYRIC OPERA *OPERA*

Founded in 1976 and based at the Shubert Theatre, the city's primary opera company offers repertory runs from standards like *Carmen* and *Madame Butterfly* to lesser-known works like *The Ballad of Baby Doe*.

 C2 Ⓐ42 SHUBERT THEATRE, 265 TREMONT ST.
617-542-4912 WWW.BLO.ORG

CHARLES PLAYHOUSE *THEATER*

A primary setting for off-Broadway productions in Boston – Blue Man Group and *Shear Madness* have both enjoyed long runs here – the theater has also served stints as a church, a synagogue, a YWCA, and a Prohibition-era speakeasy.

 C2 Ⓐ41 74 WARRENTON ST.
617-426-6912 AND 617-426-5225
WWW.BLUEMAN.COM
WWW.SHEARMADNESS.COM/BOSTON.PHP

COLONIAL THEATRE *THEATER*

Built in 1900 and holding 1,700, Boston's oldest continuously running theater is the cornerstone of the Broadway in Boston program, which brings the best of touring blockbusters to the area.

 B2 Ⓐ23 106 BOYLSTON ST.
617-426-9366 WWW.BROADWAYINBOSTON.COM

COMMONWEALTH SHAKESPEARE CO. *THEATER*

Come midsummer, this theater group puts on the annual Shakespeare on the Common (Boston Common, that is) event, performing one of the bard's plays under the stars for free.

 B2 Ⓐ21 BOSTON COMMON NEAR THE PARKMAN BANDSTAND
617-532-1252 WWW.FREESHAKESPEARE.ORG

BOSTON LYRIC OPERA

COMMONWEALTH SHAKESPEARE CO.

THE OPERA HOUSE *OPERA*

Boston's newest venue is also one of its oldest. Built as a vaudeville palace in the 1920s, the Opera House has gone through various transformations and now is a venue for the Broadway in Boston program and the Boston Ballet's *The Nutcracker.*

 B3 A 32 539 WASHINGTON ST.
617-259-3400 WWW.BROADWAYINBOSTON.COM

ORPHEUM THEATRE *CONCERTS*

Tucked away on a dead-end street, the smallish entrance belies the grand-but-worn theater within. Debuting in 1852 as a music hall, it remains true to its roots as an alternative to arena rock and roll, drawing top bands and musicians.

 B3 A 24 HAMILTON PLACE
617-679-0810 WWW.LIVENATION.COM

STUART STREET PLAYHOUSE *THEATER*

Housed in the Radisson Hotel, the playhouse stages long-running off-Broadway hits like *Stomp* and *Menopause: The Musical.*

 C1 A 40 RADISSON HOTEL BOSTON, 200 STUART ST.
617-426-4499 WWW.STUARTSTREETPLAYHOUSE.COM

WANG CENTER FOR THE PERFORMING ARTS *VARIOUS*

The nucleus of Boston's performing arts scene, the center includes the Wang Theatre, which hosts top musical theater, and the Shubert Theatre, home to Boston Lyric Opera. It is also a venue for the Bank of Boston Celebrity Series.

 C2 A 46 270 TREMONT ST.
617-482-9393 WWW.WANGCENTER.ORG

WILBUR THEATRE *THEATER*

Another of the Broadway in Boston theaters, this Federal Revival-style, 1,200-seat theater features touring and pre-Broadway shows. Plays shown here include *The Tale of the Allergist's Wife* and *Defending the Caveman.*

 C2 A 43 246 TREMONT ST.
617-423-4008 WWW.BROADWAYINBOSTON.COM

 BACK BAY/SOUTH END

BERKLEE PERFORMANCE CENTER *CONCERTS*

Once an opulent movie theater, the Berklee College of Music's center hosts about 200 events a year, from student concerts and songwriter festivals to bigger-ticket draws, including rock, folk, and jazz stars.

 C2 A 35 136 MASSACHUSETTS AVE.
617-747-2261 WWW.BERKLEEBPC.COM

BOSTON CENTER FOR THE ARTS *THEATER*

Housed in a four-acre complex, the BCA comprises three small theaters (and four theater companies in residence) as well as the landmark Cyclorama, a 23,000-square-foot rotunda. Events include theater, concerts, poetry readings, and special events. The center also includes the Mills Gallery, which showcases avant-garde art and installations.

 E5 A 71 539 TREMONT ST.
617-426-2787 WWW.BCAONLINE.ORG

EMMANUEL MUSIC *CONCERTS*

This music ensemble was formed to present the 200-plus Bach sacred cantatas in a liturgical setting. Today, it continues to perform classical music at historic Emmanuel Church, possessor of one of the world's largest pipe organs.

 B6 A 28 15 NEWBURY ST.
617-536-3356 WWW.EMMANUELMUSIC.ORG

LYRIC STAGE CO. *THEATER*

Taking residence in a 240-seat theater on the second floor of the YWCA building, this group presents a series of off-Broadway fare, including regional premieres.

 C5 A 53 140 CLARENDON ST.
617-585-5678 WWW.LYRICSTAGE.COM

MAP 5 FENWAY/KENMORE SQUARE

BOSTON SYMPHONY ORCHESTRA/SYMPHONY HALL *CLASSICAL MUSIC*

Home to both the storied Boston Symphony Orchestra and its popular sister group, the lighter Boston Pops, the Italian Renaissance-style hall doesn't have a bad seat among all 2,000 plus.

 E6 A 33 301 MASSACHUSETTS AVE.
617-266-1492 WWW.BSO.ORG

HUNTINGTON THEATRE CO. *THEATER*

Affiliated with Boston University, this company focuses on bringing new American plays to the stage while still showcasing classics at the 890-seat Boston University Theatre. The company also

TSAI PERFORMANCE CENTER

BRATTLE THEATRE

performs in a 360-seat theater at the Calderwood Pavilion at the Boston Center for the Arts.

 F6 Ⓐ 39 264 HUNTINGTON AVE.
617-266-0800 WWW.HUNTINGTONTHEATRE.ORG

NEW ENGLAND CONSERVATORY *CONCERTS*
The United States' oldest independent school of music offers some 600 shows a year. Primarily performing in Jordan Hall, itself a national historic landmark, the NEC is a force in opera and jazz.

 F6 Ⓐ 38 JORDAN HALL, 30 GAINSBOROUGH ST.
617-585-1260, 617585-1100
WWW.NEWENGLANDCONSERVATORY.EDU

TSAI PERFORMANCE CENTER *VARIOUS*
This Boston University-affiliated center with an advanced acoustic system hosts the New England Philharmonic and other classical concerts as well as dance and special events.

 B3 Ⓐ 2 BOSTON UNIVERSITY, 685 COMMONWEALTH AVE.
617-353-8725 WWW.BU.EDU/TSAI

MAP 6 CAMBRIDGE/HARVARD SQUARE

AMERICAN REPERTORY THEATRE *THEATER*
This progressive theater – both a resident acting company and a training conservatory – premieres works by up-and-coming and big-name playwrights such as David Mamet, Don DeLillo, and Paula Vogel.

MAP 6 C2 Ⓐ 5 64 BRATTLE ST.
617-547-8300 WWW.AMREP.ORG

BRATTLE THEATRE *MOVIE HOUSE*
A film buff's popcorn-scented nirvana, this Harvard Square institution shows films and film series from all genres and hosts events and lectures.

 D3 Ⓐ 21 40 BRATTLE ST.
617-876-6837 WWW.BRATTLEFILM.ORG

HARVARD FILM ARCHIVE *MOVIE HOUSE*

With nightly screenings, the HFA features both classic and obscure movies from its huge collection. Series themes run from serious ("The Vietnam War on Film") to subjective ("People We Like: Harvey Keitel"). Directors often speak at screenings.

MAP 6 D5 A 37 HARVARD UNIVERSITY, 24 QUINCY ST.
617-495-4700 WWW.HARVARDFILMARCHIVE.ORG

JOSÉ MATEO'S BALLET THEATRE *DANCE*

José Mateo's risk-taking professional ballet troupe makes its home in an old, still-functioning church in Harvard Square. Its interpretation of *The Nutcracker* is performed annually at the Sanctuary Theatre.

MAP 6 E4 A 51 400 HARVARD ST.
617-354-7467 WWW.BALLETTHEATRE.ORG

SANDERS THEATRE *VARIOUS*

Located in the venerable Memorial Hall, this historic theater offers great acoustics for music groups such as the Boston Chamber Music Society and Christmas Revels and for performers like Dave Brubeck and Joan Baez.

 D5 A 35 HARVARD UNIVERSITY, 45 QUINCY ST.
617-496-2222
WWW.FAS.HARVARD.EDU

OVERVIEW MAP

BANK OF AMERICA PAVILION *CONCERTS*

A waterfront amphitheater with Boston's harbor and skyline as a backdrop, the pavilion offers an A-list selection of rock and pop acts – think Anita Baker, Bonnie Raitt, Ringo Starr, and Elvis Costello – from May through September.

OVERVIEW MAP **D6** SOUTH BOSTON, 290 NORTHERN AVE.
617-728-1600
HTTP://BANKOFAMERICAPAVILION.COM

COOLIDGE CORNER THEATRE *MOVIE HOUSE*

This independent movie house packs them into its art deco space for indie flicks, film series, singalongs to old favorites, and themed midnight movies on weekends.

OVERVIEW MAP **E1** BROOKLINE, 290 HARVARD ST.
617-734-2500 WWW.COOLIDGE.ORG

SOMERVILLE THEATRE *VARIOUS*

Opened in 1914 as a vaudeville house, the Somerville Theatre still has a diverse entertainment heritage, offering big singer-songwriter acts and second-run and indie films on the cheap.

OVERVIEW MAP **A1** SOMERVILLE, 55 DAVIS SQUARE
617-625-5700
WWW.SOMERVILLETHEATREONLINE.COM

RECREATION

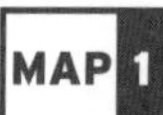 NORTH END/GOVERNMENT CENTER

CHRISTOPHER COLUMBUS PARK

For a great picnic, grab a sandwich at nearby Faneuil Hall and head to this waterfront park. A lovely little rose garden here is dedicated to Kennedy family matriarch Rose Fitzgerald Kennedy, who was born nearby.

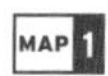 F5 54 ATLANTIC AVE. AT COMMERCIAL WHARF

 BEACON HILL

COMMUNITY BOATING

Boston visitors can explore the Charles River through short-term Community Boating memberships; with two-day memberships, experienced sailors can ply the river on Mercury sailboats and paddlers can venture out in kayaks.

  8 THE ESPLANADE BTWN. HATCH SHELL AND LONGFELLOW BRIDGE
617-523-1038 WWW.COMMUNITY-BOATING.ORG

THE ESPLANADE

Start at the Hatch Shell, and jog, bike, or skate down this park's path that winds along the Boston side of the Charles. For the more languorous, a ride on one of the Venetian-style gondolas is the way to go, though reservations are highly recommended.

  10 SOUTH CHARLES RIVER BANK BTWN. LONGFELLOW BRIDGE AND HARVARD BRIDGE
617-876-2800 WWW.BOSTONGONDOLAS.COM
WWW.MASS.GOV

MAP 3 DOWNTOWN/CHINATOWN

BOSTON COMMON

See SIGHTS, p. 7.

MAP 3 A2 2 BTWN. CHARLES AND TREMONT STS., BEACON AND BOYLSTON STS.

 **BOSTON HARBOR ISLANDS**

Take a ferry to one of these 34 islands, which offer swimming,

BOSTON COMMON

BACK BAY FENS

hiking, and camping. The most popular is George's Island, where Confederate prisoners were held captive during the Civil War.

 A6 15 FERRIES FROM LONG WHARF
617-223-8666 WWW.NPS.GOV/BOHA

BOSTON HARBORWALK

Since 1984, the Boston Harbor Association has been working to establish public access to Boston Harbor via a self-guided walk from East Boston and Charlestown through downtown over the Fort Point Channel to South Boston. About 80 percent of the 47 miles of waterfront is now accessible.

 D5 57 253 SUMMER ST. ALONG THE FORT POINT CHANNEL
617-482-1722 WWW.BOSTONHARBORWALK.COM

PUBLIC GARDEN

See SIGHTS, p. 7.

 B1 16 BTWN. ARLINGTON AND CHARLES STS., BEACON AND BOYLSTON STS.

SWAN BOATS

From April to September, catamaran Swan Boats – made famous in *Make Way for Ducklings* – ply the waters of the Public Garden's lagoon alongside mallards and, yes, real swans.

 A1 1 PUBLIC GARDEN, NEAR CHARLES ST.
617-591-1150 WWW.SWANBOATS.COM

MAP 4 BACK BAY/SOUTH END

BOSTON DUCK TOURS

Explore Boston's sights inside a reconditioned World War II amphibious craft. With mandatory group quacking and a splash into the Charles River, these 80-minute tours live up to their advance billing.

 C3 37 START AT PRUDENTIAL CENTER, 800 BOYLSTON ST.
617-267-3825 WWW.BOSTONDUCKTOURS.COM

HARBOR EXCURSIONS

One of the best ways to see Boston is to leave its shores entirely and venture into the famous (and infamously maligned) Boston Harbor. You might ply its now-clean waters with a variety of boat tours, ranging from whale-watching excursions to mystery and music cruises, including those offered by the ***Spirit of Boston*** (866-211-3807, www.spiritofboston.com), **Massachusetts Bay Lines** (617-542-8000 www.massbaylines.com), and **Boston Harbor Cruises** (617-227-4321, www.bostonharborcruises.com). The **New England Aquarium (p. 9)** also offers whale-watching excursions and both daytime and sunset cruises. You might also explore the harbor by visiting one of the 34 islands that make up the **Boston Harbor Islands (p. 73),** a national park area.

FENWAY/KENMORE SQUARE

BACK BAY FENS

One of the prettiest marshes you'll see, these 113 acres of gardens, sculpted hedges, flower beds, and paths make up one link in Boston's five-mile chain of urban parks known as the Emerald Necklace.

 E5 32 ENTRANCE AT WESTLAND AVE. AT HEMENWAY ST.
617-635-4505 OR 617-232-5374
WWW.EMERALDNECKLACE.ORG

FENWAY PARK

See SIGHTS, p. 12.

 D4 22 4 YAWKEY WAY
617-267-9440

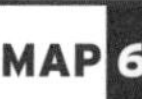

CAMBRIDGE/HARVARD SQUARE

CHESS IN HARVARD SQUARE

You don't have to be a chess master to grab a seat in Cambridge's Harvard Square and battle pawns, knights, and rooks against a stranger. Spectators can have just as much fun watching from the sidelines.

 D3 27 HARVARD SQUARE, MASSACHUSETTS AVE. AT JOHN F. KENNEDY ST.

JOHN F. KENNEDY PARK

With its view of the Charles River, this park honoring Boston's favorite son is an ideal place to picnic. A fountain is engraved with

JOHN F. KENNEDY PARK

ARNOLD ARBORETUM

excerpts from a 1961 Kennedy speech that are as distinctively Bostonian as Kennedy's own accent.

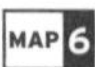 E1 Ⓐ 39 MEMORIAL DR. AT JOHN F. KENNEDY ST.

OFF MAP

ARNOLD ARBORETUM

One of the country's oldest gardens, the Arnold Arboretum covers its 265 acres with some 4,500 varieties of shrubs, trees, plants, and vines and exudes the perfume of azaleas, dogwoods, lilacs, and rhododendrons.

OFF MAP JAMAICA PLAIN, 125 ARBORWAY
617-524-1718 WWW.ARBORETUM.HARVARD.EDU

FRANKLIN PARK ZOO

An institution since 1913, the zoo features a tropical forest, a hands-on farm, a seasonal butterfly house, as well as lions, tigers, giraffes, and gorillas.

OFF MAP JAMAICA PLAIN, 1 FRANKLIN PARK RD.
617-541-5466 WWW.FRANKLINPARKZOO.ORG

REVERE BEACH

America's first public beach is just five miles north of the city and a quick train ride away. The bandstand, the people-watching, and the overstuffed sandwiches from Kelly's Roast Beef are all reasons to make the trip.

OFF MAP REVERE, REVERE BEACH PKWY.
781-438-1388
WWW.MASS.GOV

HOTELS

Trendsetter favorite: **NINE ZERO,** p. 80

Most romantic: **LENOX HOTEL,** p. 82

Best-value boutique hotel: **CHARLESMARK,** p. 80

Grandest lobby for a rendezvous:
FAIRMONT COPLEY PLAZA, p. 82

Best views: **BOSTON HARBOR HOTEL,** p. 79

Best place to be pampered:
RITZ-CARLTON, BOSTON COMMON, p. 80

Best you-only-live-once splurge:
FOUR SEASONS HOTEL BOSTON, p. 79

PRICE KEY

$ ROOMS UNDER $200

$$ ROOMS $200-300

$$$ ROOMS OVER $300

MAP 1 NORTH END/GOVERNMENT CENTER

BULFINCH HOTEL *CHIC $$*

This nine-story former industrial building has been transformed into a sleek boutique hotel with minimalist furnishings and high-speed Internet. The 80 guest rooms vary in size due to the building's triangular shape.

MAP 1 D2 H7 107 MERRIMAC ST.
617-624-0202 WWW.BULFINCHHOTEL.COM

HARBORSIDE HOTEL *ROMANTIC $*

Built as a warehouse in 1858, this newly renovated 98-room hotel a block from Faneuil Hall offers old-Boston charm in a modern setting, including flat-screen TVs and iPod docs in the guest rooms. The rooms aren't large, but some overlook the skylit atrium while better ones have city views.

MAP 1 F4 H52 185 STATE ST.
617-723-7500 WWW.HARBORSIDEINNBOSTON.COM

MILLENNIUM BOSTONIAN *ROMANTIC $$*

Request a room with a fireplace in the old-world Boston Harkness Wing built in 1824. The newer wing is decorated in light woods with balconies. For a quieter night, stay in a room facing away from the street.

MAP 1 E3 H29 26 NORTH ST.
617-523-3600 OR 866-866-8086
WWW.MILLENNIUMHOTELS.COM/BOSTON

ONYX HOTEL *CHIC $$*

Fashionable red suede chairs, black desks, and taupe walls adorn this luxury boutique hotel. All rooms have plush linens, flat-screen TVs, and Aveda bath products. Request morning car service to the Financial District weekdays.

MAP 1 D2 H8 155 PORTLAND ST.
617-557-9955 OR 866-660-6699 WWW.ONYXHOTEL.COM

MAP 2 BEACON HILL

BEACON HILL HOTEL AND BISTRO *CHIC $$*

Two townhouses were renovated to make way for a 13-room hotel fashioned in cool neutral tones and minimalist decor. Escape to the hidden roof deck overlooking Charles Street for an afternoon cocktail.

H33 25 CHARLES ST.
617-723-7575 OR 888-959-2442
WWW.BEACONHILLHOTEL.COM

CHARLES STREET INN *ROMANTIC $$*

This 1860s townhouse has been converted into a deluxe inn. All nine Victorian rooms have working fireplaces, and period details include canopy and four-poster beds, roll-top desks, and fainting couches.

H14 94 CHARLES ST.
617-314-8900 OR 877-772-8900
WWW.CHARLESSTREETINN.COM

CHARLES STREET INN

XV BEACON

XV BEACON *CHIC* *$$$*

Sophisticated style and over-the-top elegance surround this luxury boutique hotel with its contemporary furnishings. Rooms are filled with high-tech amenities and some include gas fireplaces and whirlpools. A chauffeured Lexus transports guests around town.

 F6 Ⓗ42 15 BEACON ST.
617-670-1500 OR 877-XVBEACON WWW.XVBEACON.COM

HOTEL MARLOWE *CHIC* *$$*

Cranberry velvet upholstered lounge chairs, jaguar-print pillows, faux-fur throws, and plenty of bold colors make this upscale 236-room, pet-friendly hotel stand out. Don't miss the complimentary wine hour in the lobby.

 A3 Ⓗ2 CAMBRIDGE, 25 EDWIN H. LAND BLVD.
617-868-8000 OR 800-825-7140
WWW.HOTELMARLOWE.COM

ROYAL SONESTA HOTEL *ROMANTIC* *$$*

After shopping at the Galleria Mall across the street, retreat to this East Cambridge hotel located across the Charles River from Beacon Hill. The panoramic city views give it a romantic feel.

 A3 Ⓗ1 CAMBRIDGE, 40 EDWIN H. LAND BLVD.
617-806-4200 OR 800-766-3782
WWW.ROYALSONESTABOSTON.COM

MAP 3 DOWNTOWN/CHINATOWN

BOSTON HARBOR HOTEL *GRAND* *$$$*

There's no better place for a room with a view than this waterfront hotel. This impressive hotel offers 230 modern rooms, many with separate sitting areas. Look for the city's Wine Expo series here each winter.

 B6 Ⓗ38 70 ROWES WHARF
617-439-7000 OR 800-752-7077 WWW.BHH.COM

FOUR SEASONS HOTEL BOSTON *GRAND* *$$$*

This class act is revered for its top-of-the-line service. The city's only five-diamond property also hosts the city's only five-diamond restaurant. Have a drink in the Bristol Lounge where you might sit next to a rock star.

MAP 3 B1 H 19 200 BOYLSTON ST.
617-338-4400 WWW.FOURSEASONS.COM/BOSTON

MARRIOTT'S CUSTOM HOUSE *GRAND* $$

Step inside Faneuil Hall's Custom House Tower and enjoy a night in the all-suite property with classic separate living and dining areas. Be sure not to miss the 26th-floor open-air observation deck.

MAP 3 A5 H 14 3 MCKINLEY SQUARE
617-310-6300 OR 800-845-5279
HTTP://MARRIOTT.COM

NINE ZERO *CHIC* $$

Swanky, chic, and contemporary describe this luxury property near Boston Common. All 190 rooms are cool with CD players, Internet access, and other amenities to please the style-conscious road warrior.

MAP 3 A4 H 7 90 TREMONT ST.
617-772-5800 OR 866-NINEZERO WWW.NINEZERO.COM

OMNI PARKER HOUSE *QUAINT* $$

America's longest continuously operating hotel (since 1855) boasts a wood-paneled lobby more elaborate than the modest rooms. Stop by Parker's restaurant where JFK proposed to Jacqueline Bouvier and where Boston cream pie was perfected.

MAP 3 A4 H 9 60 SCHOOL ST.
617-227-8600 OR 800-843-6664
WWW.PARKERHOUSEBOSTON.COM

RITZ-CARLTON, BOSTON COMMON *GRAND* $$$

This contemporary, marble-and-glass tower overlooking Boston Common epitomizes opulent Boston. The chain's impeccable service includes 24-hour attention and bath menu options. The neutral rooms have a muted elegance, each with a breathtaking view.

MAP 3 B3 H 30 10 AVERY ST.
617-574-7100 OR 800-241-3333
WWW.RITZCARLTON.COM/HOTELS/BOSTON_COMMON

MAP 4 BACK BAY/SOUTH END

BOSTON PARK PLAZA *GRAND* $$$

Built in 1927, this landmark property always bustles with tourists and business travelers. The nearly 950 rooms are tastefully decorated; concierge-level rooms are a bit larger than standard and provide access to the Towers Lounge.

MAP 4 C6 H 58 64 ARLINGTON ST.
617-426-2000 WWW.BOSTONPARKPLAZA.COM

CHARLESMARK *CHIC* $$

Located at the finish line of the Boston Marathon, this boutique property is the trademark of a modestly priced hotel. Local artwork

NINE ZERO

CLARENDON SQUARE INN

lines the halls leading to 40 modern rooms smartly outfitted with high-tech gadgets.

 B4 H19 655 BOYLSTON ST.
617-247-1212 WWW.CHARLESMARKHOTEL.COM

CLARENDON SQUARE INN *CHIC* $$
Each of the three rooms in this classy brownstone is uniquely furnished to ensure a luxurious and comfortable stay. All have wood-burning fireplaces and queen beds while the rooftop hot tub has fine city views.

 E4 H68 198 W. BROOKLINE ST.
617-536-2229 WWW.CLARENDONSQUARE.COM

THE COLLEGE CLUB *QUAINT* $
You don't have to be a member to stay at this aristocratic women's club. There are 11 guest rooms in the Victorian brownstone and although the shared-bath singles are like dorm rooms, the doubles with private bath are spacious.

 B6 H25 44 COMMONWEALTH AVE.
617-536-9510 WWW.THECOLLEGECLUBOFBOSTON.COM

COLONNADE HOTEL *GRAND* $$
Directly across from the Prudential Center, the '60s-era concrete exterior belies the traditionally appointed rooms that offer floor-to-ceiling windows and a view of the city. The rooftop pool is a secret oasis in the summer.

 D3 H61 120 HUNTINGTON AVE.
617-424-7000 OR 800-962-3030
WWW.COLONNADEHOTEL.COM

COPLEY SQUARE HOTEL *ROMANTIC* $$
The 142 rooms at one of the city's oldest hotels are all different – some are prim with floral bedspreads, while others are simply dressed. The convenient Back Bay location is a standout with tourists.

 C4 H46 47 HUNTINGTON AVE.
617-536-9000 OR 800-225-7062
WWW.COPLEYSQUAREHOTEL.COM

82 CHANDLER STREET B&B *QUAINT* $
This charming brick townhouse – with three Victorian-style guest rooms and two studio apartments – is decorated in lively colors. The top-floor room, with a working fireplace, is the finest.

 D5 H65 82 CHANDLER ST.
617-482-0408 OR 888-482-0408
WWW.82CHANDLER.COM

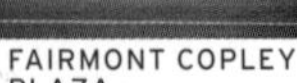
FAIRMONT COPLEY PLAZA

HOTEL COMMONWEALTH

ENCORE BED & BREAKFAST *CHIC* $

Calling itself an "anti-antique B&B," this classic townhouse has three airy, artsy contemporary guest rooms strikingly decorated with rich colors and a mix of retro and modern furnishings. Continental breakfast includes pastries, fruit, and granola.

MAP 4 E4 H 69
116 W. NEWTON ST.
617-247-3425 WWW.ENCOREBANDB.COM

FAIRMONT COPLEY PLAZA *GRAND* $$$

Boston's Grande Dame offers 366 classically inspired accommodations (each with a marble bath) with one of the most lavish lobbies in town. The Fairmont Gold offers an ultra club level with private lounge, dining room, and library.

MAP 4 C5 H 51
138 ST. JAMES AVE.
617-267-5300 OR 866-540-4417
WWW.FAIRMONT.COM/COPLEYPLAZA

JURYS BOSTON HOTEL *GRAND* $$

An Irish hotel group transformed the former Boston Police headquarters into a 222-room luxury property. The 1925 historic structure now features comfortable guest rooms with WiFi and an on-site coffee bar and Irish pub.

MAP 4 C5 H 54
350 STUART ST.
617-266-7200 WWW.JURYSDOYLE.COM

LENOX HOTEL *ROMANTIC* $$$

This plush, old-school hotel is bedecked with chandeliers, blue hallways, and period details of its century-old structure. Rooms have marble baths and custom-made furnishings. For a memorable evening, request a corner room with working fireplace.

MAP 4 C4 H 41
61 EXETER ST.
617-536-5300 OR 800-225-7676 WWW.LENOXHOTEL.COM

NEWBURY GUEST HOUSE *QUAINT* $

These three interconnected side-by-side brownstones offer great value on the city's most fashionable street. The 32 simple rooms are furnished with Victorian reproductions and Oriental-style rugs. The prettiest have bay windows; some have fireplaces.

MAP 4 B3 H 10
261 NEWBURY ST.
617-437-7666 WWW.NEWBURYGUESTHOUSE.COM

THE WESTIN COPLEY PLACE *GRAND $$*
This 36-story property offers more than 800 spacious and stylish rooms. Guests can take advantage of on-site meeting facilities, unwind at the indoor pool and spa, or dine at the on-site steakhouse and sushi lounge.

MAP 4 C4 H 47 10 HUNTINGTON AVE.
617-262-9600 OR 800-937-8461 WWW.WESTIN.COM

MAP 5 FENWAY/KENMORE SQUARE

BUCKMINSTER *QUAINT $*
This budget hotel, located at the intersection of Beacon Street and Brookline Avenue, serves an eclectic clientele of European students, Boston University parents, and club kids. The basic rooms vary from tiny to quite comfortable.

MAP 5 C4 H 3 645 BEACON ST.
617-236-7050 WWW.BOSTONHOTELBUCKMINSTER.COM

ELIOT HOTEL *ROMANTIC $$$*
This circa-1925 neo-Georgian boutique property features 95 rooms and suites appointed with luxe marble bathrooms, Egyptian linens, and WiFi. Room service from much-revered Clio is available around the clock.

MAP 5 D6 H 28 370 COMMONWEALTH AVE.
617-267-1607 OR 800-443-5468 WWW.ELIOTHOTEL.COM

HOTEL COMMONWEALTH *GRAND $$$*
This elegant six-story newcomer in the heart of Kenmore Square offers guest rooms with luxurious amenities such as Italian linens and marble bathrooms. Request one of the Fenway rooms, which face the legendary ballpark.

MAP 5 C5 H 18 500 COMMONWEALTH AVE.
617-933-5000 OR 866-784-4000
WWW.HOTELCOMMONWEALTH.COM

MAP 6 CAMBRIDGE/HARVARD SQUARE

CHARLES HOTEL *GRAND $$$*
The contemporary Shaker-style furniture and handmade quilts of this Harvard Square gem suggests simple luxury. Ask for a room on the seventh floor or higher for a river or skyline view.

MAP 6 D2 H 18 1 BENNETT ST.
617-864-1200 OR 800-882-1818
WWW.CHARLESHOTEL.COM

HARVARD SQUARE HOTEL *QUAINT $$*
A recent facelift provided each of the 73 rooms with new carpet and oak furniture. Situated above a parking lot, this four-story

hotel may resemble a college dorm, but the updated rooms are comfortable and affordable.

MAP 6 D2 H 13 110 MT. AUBURN ST.
617-864-5200 WWW.HARVARDSQUAREHOTEL.COM

INN AT HARVARD *QUAINT $$*

Located adjacent to Harvard Yard, this Georgian-style brick hotel was built around a "living room" atrium covered with ivy. Inside, it mixes sketches on loan from the local Fogg Art Museum with contemporary art.

MAP 6 E4 H 50 1201 MASSACHUSETTS AVE.
617-491-2222 OR 800-458-5886
WWW.THEINNATHARVARD.COM

IRVING HOUSE *QUAINT $*

This 44-room rambling Victorian is a bit pricey for its somewhat small but otherwise homey rooms (including some shared baths). Its location on a peaceful residential street close to Harvard Square make it worth a stay.

MAP 6 D6 H 38 24 IRVING ST.
617-547-4600 OR 877-547-4600
WWW.IRVINGHOUSE.COM

SHERATON COMMANDER *QUAINT $$*

This stately brick building dates to 1927 and is named for America's first commander in chief – honoring when Washington took command of the Continental Army at Cambridge Common. The colonial-style rooms with canopy beds recall the Revolutionary era.

MAP 6 B3 H 3 16 GARDEN ST.
617-547-4800 WWW.SHERATONCOMMANDER.COM

OVERVIEW MAP

HOTEL @ MIT *CHIC $$*

Adjacent to tech powerhouse MIT, this Hilton property offers its gadget-loving guests in-room WiFi, Sony PlayStations, laptop safes, and networked laser printing. Low-tech touches include earth-toned decor, high-thread-count linens, and Aveda bath products.

OVERVIEW MAP C3 20 SIDNEY ST.
617-577-0200 OR 800-222-8733
WWW.HOTELATMIT.COM

HYATT REGENCY CAMBRIDGE *GRAND $$*

The off-the-beaten-path location offers a tranquility often lacking in urban hotels. Take a ride on the glass elevators up 16 floors and request a room with a balcony that overlooks the atrium or upgrade to one with an outdoor sundeck.

OVERVIEW MAP C5 575 MEMORIAL DR.
617-492-1234 OR 888-591-1234
WWW.CAMBRIDGE.HYATT.COM

CITY ESSENTIALS

AIRPORT

Many private and public transportation options exist from Boston's Logan International Airport (800-235-6426, www.massport.com/logan), which is located in East Boston, about 3.5 miles from downtown. It is almost a city unto itself, with its own state police troop, Fire Rescue Unit, and nondenominational chapel. A drive to or from downtown can take 20-40 minutes, depending on Boston's famous traffic. The Massachusetts Port Authority (Massport) runs free shuttles that provide service between the airline terminal arrival areas to the nearest subway station. Logan Express offers convenient bus service from four suburban locations: Braintree (south), Framingham (west), and Peabody and Woburn (north). Round-trip tickets are $20 and on-site parking is $11 per day.

The new MBTA Silver Line offers the cheapest and best direct connection to and from South Station. One-way fares are just $1.25. The MBTA Blue Line, which is easily accessible from all MBTA and commuter rail stations, has an Airport Station train stop and provides free shuttles to all airline terminals.

Year-round water shuttles are also available to the Logan dock from direct connections to downtown Boston and other waterfront destinations. One-way tickets to Hull and Quincy on the South Shore cost $6 aboard Harbor Express. If you are staying at the Seaport Hotel, Marriott Long Wharf, or Residence Inn, call City Water Taxi for a direct connection from the hotel (one-way fares $10). The Rowes Wharf Water Taxi provides taxi service from a variety of downtown locations (one-way fares $10). Many boat services run among Boston harbor's handful of wharves, including the following: Long Wharf, Lovejoy, Charlestown Navy Yard, Courthouse, World Trade Center, Rowes Wharf, and the suburban South Shore Wharf at Hingham Harbor.

Taxis are found on the arrival levels of each terminal 24 hours a day. Within a 12-mile radius of downtown Boston, taxis charge a metered rate. Beyond that range, they charge a flat rate. A $1.50 fee is applied to all fares leaving the airport. Also expect a $4.50 toll fee for fares to Boston that travel through the harbor tunnels. The average price of a trip downtown from the airport is $20, including tip and tolls. Flat fees for longer distances depend on your final destination and can run from $30 on up.

CITY WATER TAXI 617-422-0392

HARBOR EXPRESS 617-222-6999

LOGAN EXPRESS 800-235-6426

MASSPORT 800-235-6426

MBTA 617-222-5215

ROWES WHARF WATER TAXI 617-406-8584

ARRIVING BY TRAIN

Bostonians like to refer to their city as the "hub of the universe," and the gateway to the city is through South Station. There is a taxi stand on Atlantic Avenue (exit at the main doors near McDonald's); rates are $1.75 for the first 1/8th mile or less with $0.30 for each additional 1/8th of a mile.

AMTRAK 800-872-7245, www.amtrak.com

MBTA/COMMUTER RAIL 617-222-5000 OR 800-392-6100, www.mbta.com

SOUTH STATION

 C4 1 SOUTH STATION, AT INTERSECTION OF SUMMER ST. AND ATLANTIC AVE. 617-330-1230

PUBLIC TRANSPORTATION

The Massachusetts Bay Transportation Authority (MBTA) provides more than a million trips daily on its bus, train, and boat network. The nation's oldest subway system, known to locals as "The T," offers cheap and easy transportation on four subway lines in and around the city. There are 13 commuter rail lines, five boat routes, and 170 bus rounds that provide service to 175 cities and towns in Massachusetts. Train service begins around 5:30 A.M. and operates until midnight. Trains on the red and green lines can be counted on to arrive every few minutes, whereas the orange and blue lines can be more sporadic, so be sure to check www.mbta.com for T line and bus information. Visitors can also purchase MBTA passes online. Regular bus service aboard the Plymouth & Brockton Bus can also take you from downtown Boston to Cape Cod.

C&J TRAILWAYS 800-258-7111, www.cjtrailways.com

CONCORD TRAILWAYS 800-639-3317, www.concordtrailways.com

DARTMOUTH COACH 800-637-0123, www.concordtrailways.com/dartmouth_coach.htm

MBTA 617-222-5215, www.mbta.com

PETER PAN BONANZA 401-751-8800 OR 888-751-8800, www.bonanzabus.com, www.peterpanbus.com

PLYMOUTH & BROCKTON STREET RAILWAY 508-746-0378, www.p-b.com

TAXIS

Taxis are easily available throughout Boston. Within a 12-mile radius of downtown Boston, taxis charge a metered rate. Beyond that range, they charge a flat rate. Also expect a $4.50 toll fee for fares to Boston that travel through the harbor tunnels.

AVIS STATE RED CAB 617-566-5000

BOSTON CAB 617-536-5010

CHECKER CAB 617-536-7000

CITY CAB 617-536-5100

INDEPENDENT TAXI OPERATORS ASSOCIATION 617-426-8700

ITOA 617-825-4000

JC TRANSPORTATION 781-598-3433 OR 800-517-2281

METRO CAB 617-782-5500 OR 617-242-8000

PEOPLE'S CHOICE TRANSPORATION 617-746-9909 OR 888-222-5229

TOWN TAXI 617-536-5000

TUNNEL TAXI 617-567-2700

DRIVING AND RENTING A CAR

For those new to Boston, just remember the rumors, while exaggerated, are mostly true: Driving in Boston can be (depending on whom you ask) either a blood sport or an art form. The Big Dig (Boston's epic central-artery construction project) has only further complicated the city's layout, creating streets that are one way one day and blocked off the next. The tunnel construction was completed in 2005, but the park construction will take more time, possibly extending through 2007. Check the Massachusetts Turnpike Authority website for details and updates at www.masspike.com.

If you do need access to your own car, you'll find plenty of major rental companies at Logan Airport. Most major car-rental companies are located in one central area at the airport. A free shuttle bus runs frequently between the airport terminals and the center. The following companies also have locations in or near downtown Boston:

ALAMO 800-462-5266, www.alamo.com

AVIS 800-831-2847, www.avis.com

BUDGET 800-527-7000, www.budget.com

DOLLAR 800-800-3665, www.dollar.com

ENTERPRISE 800-264-6350, www.enterprise.com

HERTZ 800-704-4473, www.hertz.com

NATIONAL 800-227-7368, www.national.com

There are numerous electronic parking meters offering two hours of on-street parking in Boston but finding a vacant one can be a challenge. The efficient public transportation system and the abundance of taxis make driving purely optional. Public parking garages are available in every neighborhood, but hourly rates can be extremely high. Residential neighborhoods require permit parking decals, and hefty orange tickets are displayed on windshields for those without one. Be sure to learn the regulations during a snow emergency or it can cost you a significant fine.

VISITOR INFORMATION

Located at Copley Place, the Greater Boston Convention & Visitors Bureau dispenses maps, guidebooks, and information on what's happening in the city. The BostonUSA Specials! Visitor Card offers discounts to museums, fitness centers, spas, restaurants, shops, performances, and sightseeing tours. Arts Boston offers BosTix locations throughout the city where you can purchase day-of-show tickets for half price.

ARTS BOSTON

MAP 4 D5 325 COLUMBUS AVE.
617-262-8632
WWW.ARTSBOSTON.ORG

GREATER BOSTON CONVENTION & VISITORS BUREAU

MAP 4 C4 2 COPLEY PLACE, SUITE 105
888-SEE-BOSTON
WWW.BOSTONUSA.COM

WEATHER

Most people come to Boston to experience the wonderful change of seasons, but the weather in Boston can be very inconsistent. The city has experienced snowfall in April and mild temperatures in November. Winters are very cold here with average temperatures around 20°-30° Fahrenheit with large amounts of snow possible. Summers heat up with humidity and temperatures in the high 80s and above. July and August are typically the warmest months of the year with January and February being the coldest.

HOURS

Boston is not a late-night city. Most restaurants stop serving food around 11 P.M., with a few late-night spots serving until 1:30 A.M. All bars close their doors at 2 A.M., with last call served around 1:30 A.M. The last train leaves the station around midnight, but times vary so be sure to call ahead for exact schedules. If you're planning on stretching out the night as long as possible, it's best to hit one of the downtown or Kenmore Square-area clubs until closing. Afterward, grab a cab and hunt out one of the few late-night diners.

FESTIVALS AND EVENTS

JANUARY

First Night: For more than 30 years, more than 1.5 million people attend the First Night celebration, which showcases Boston's cultural and artistic communities with more than 250 exhibitions and performances by both local and internationally recognized artists. December 31-January 1. (Downtown, 617-542-1399, www.firstnight.org)

FEBRUARY

Anthony Spinazzola Foundation Gala Festival: The foundation hosts its annual gala celebration of food and wine to benefit Boston's homeless. Early February. (Various locations, 781-344-4413, www.spinazzola.org)

The Boston Wine Expo: The largest consumer wine event in the country offers a sampling of 1,800 wines from more than 440 wineries from across the globe. Mid-February. (Seaport World Trade Center Boston, 877-946-3976, www.wine-expos.com/boston)

MARCH

New England Spring Flower Show: The first sign of springtime in Boston is when the Massachusetts Horticultural Society hosts this annual event – going strong after more than 130 years. Mid-March. (Bayside Expo Center, 617-933-4984, www.masshort.org)

St. Patrick's Day Parade: People often joke that there are more Irish people in this city than in Ireland – what better way to celebrate than with this long-running tradition? Mid-March. (South Boston, 617-696-9880, www.saintpatricksdayparade.com/boston)

APRIL

Boston Marathon: The world's oldest – and most prestigious – annual 26-mile marathon is held on Patriot's Day, the third Monday in April. (Hopkinton to Boston, 617-236-1652, www.baa.org/bostonmarathon)

Red Sox Opening Day: Spring training is over and now it's time to catch the World Series Champion Red Sox at Opening Day. Mid-April. (Fenway Park, 617-267-9440, www.redsox.com)

MAY

Walk for Hunger: More than 40,000 people each year walk 20 miles in early May to raise money for hungry people in Massachusetts. Early May. (Downtown Boston, 617-723-5000, www.projectbread.org)

JUNE

Scooper Bowl: The nation's largest all-you-can-eat ice cream festival scoops ice cream from 10 sponsors with all proceeds benefiting The Jimmy Fund. Early June. (City Hall Plaza, 800-525-4669, www.jimmyfund.org)

JULY

Boston's Fourth of July: Up to 700,000 people attend this free event hosted by the Boston Pops, which ends in a spectacular fireworks display. July 4. (Esplanade on the Charles, 888-4TH-POPS, www.july4th.org)

AUGUST

Restaurant Week: Nearly 100 restaurants in and around the city come together to offer prix fixe menus for lunch and dinner. It's a great way to sample the best tastes of the city on a budget price. Mid-August. (Restaurants throughout Boston, 888-SEE-BOSTON, www.restaurantweekboston.com)

SEPTEMBER

Boston Film Festival: For more than 20 years, this festival has screened premieres and hosted acclaimed directors and actors, including Jodie Foster, Al Pacino, Steve Martin, Kevin Spacey, and Nicolas Cage in their debut film performances. Early-mid-September. (Loews Boston Common, 617-523-8388, www.bostonfilmfestival.org)

Boston Folk Festival: Since 1998, this annual family-friendly event has drawn folk-music fans to hear a diverse lineup of live performances. The festival features several stages, food, crafts, and activities for kids. Mid-September. (University of Massachusetts at Boston, 617-287-6911, www.bostonfolkfestival.org)

Opening Night at the Symphony: If you weren't in town for the Pops summer concert at the Esplanade, now is your chance to see them perform at Symphony Hall. Late September. (Boston Symphony Hall, 617-266-1200, www.bso.org)

OCTOBER

Harvard Square Oktoberfest: Autumn has finally arrived when Harvard Square celebrates its annual Oktoberfest with a festival of food, entertainment, and shopping. Early October. (Harvard Square, 617-491-3434, www.harvardsquare.com/oktoberfest)

Head of the Charles Regatta: Over two days, more than 7,000 athletes compete in 24 races for the honorary Head of the Charles title. Late October. (The Charles River in Cambridge, 617-868-6200, www.hocr.org)

NOVEMBER

Boston Jewish Film Festival: Visiting artists from around the world come here to introduce their films, participate in panel discussions, and answer audience questions. Early November. (Loews Boston Common, Museum of Fine Arts, and other locations, 617-244-9899, www.bjff.org)

DECEMBER

The Nutcracker: The Boston Ballet's performance of the classic story *The Nutcracker* is a holiday tradition. In 2005 the ballet company moved the performance to Boston's historic Opera House. Throughout December. (Boston Ballet, www.bostonballet.org)

Christmas Tree Lighting: More than 30,000 people gather at the Prudential Center each year for the lighting of the Boston Christmas tree. The tree is a gift from the people of Nova Scotia as a symbol of their gratitude for Boston's assistance after a 1917 munitions explosion in Halifax. Early December. (Prudential Center, 617-236-3100)

Boston Tea Party Reenactment: Visitors are invited to participate in the lively reenactment celebrating the 1773 rally against the British tea tax. Mid-December. (Old South Meeting House, www.oldsouthmeetinghouse.org)

DISABLED ACCESS

Most MBTA stations are fully accessible via street-to-concourse and street-to-platform elevators, however some stations do not provide elevators to all platforms. Braille signage assists passengers who are vision-impaired. MBTA's "The Ride" provides door-to-door transportation to eligible people who cannot use the public bus or train system. Lift-equipped vans are used to serve persons with disabilities, including those who use wheelchairs and scooters. The Ride operates every day 6 A.M.–1 A.M. in 62 cities and towns. Handicapped parking is available throughout the city, and all public buildings have been newly constructed or retrofitted to be ADA compliant and comfortably accommodate individuals with disabilities. For more information, contact the Massachusetts Network of Information Providers for People with Disabilities at 781-642-0248 or 800-642-0249 or the Massachusetts Office on Disability at 617-727-7440 and www.disabilityinfo.org.

SAFETY

As in any city, visitors to Boston should travel smart, stay alert, and take precautionary safety measures. Boston is a relatively safe city where robberies are uncommon, and security in parks and on streets is fairly tight. Car thefts have been known to happen, so use common sense and don't leave valuables in plain sight when leaving your car parked and locked. Parts of Chinatown and Downtown Crossing should be avoided at night.

HEALTH AND EMERGENCY SERVICES

For immediate emergency medical service, dial 911. If urgent medical care is required with or without the assistance of an ambulance, the following medical centers offer 24-hour emergency care:

BETH ISRAEL DEACONESS MEDICAL CENTER
MAP 5 E2 330 BROOKLINE AVE.
617-754-2400

BOSTON MEDICAL CENTER
OVERVIEW MAP E4 1 BOSTON MEDICAL CENTER PL.
617-414-4075

BRIGHAM AND WOMEN'S HOSPITAL
MAP 5 F2 75 FRANCIS ST.
617-732-5500

MASSACHUSETTS GENERAL HOSPITAL
MAP 2 D4 55 FRUIT ST.
617-726-2000

MT. AUBURN HOSPITAL
OVERVIEW MAP B1 330 MT. AUBURN ST.
617-499-5025

NEW ENGLAND MEDICAL CENTER
MAP 3 C2 830 WASHINGTON ST.
617-636-5566

PHARMACIES

CVS
MAP 2 D3 155 CHARLES ST.
617-227-0437

WALGREENS
MAP 4 C3 841 BOYLSTON ST.
617-236-8130

MEDIA AND COMMUNICATIONS

Boston's two daily newspapers, the *Boston Globe* and the *Boston Herald,* provide coverage of local, national, and international news, plus separate sections on lifestyle, food, arts, and entertainment. Four free publications, found in street bins and at some businesses, are the *Boston Phoenix, Stuff @ Night, Dig,* and the *Improper Bostonian.* All four offer entertainment and restaurant information, while the *Phoenix* also includes news and editorials. The city's monthly magazine, *Boston Magazine,* covers food, arts, entertainment, and city-related features. *Boston Common* offers a more upscale approach to the inner workings of the city. *Scene Boston* takes a peek inside the lifestyles of some famous Bostonians.

Public pay phones are not readily available around town; most are located within restaurants, transportation stations, and hotels. In Massachusetts, drivers may use mobile phones, as long as doing so does not interfere with driving and one hand stays on the wheel at all times.

Most local post office branches are open 8 A.M.-5:30 P.M. on weekdays and 8 A.M.-noon on Saturdays. You can find a centrally located post office in the Back Bay.

POST OFFICE

 390 STUART ST.
617-236-7800

INTERNET

Nearly every hotel in Boston and Cambridge offers high-speed Internet access. A few offer access as an amenity at no charge but most hotels charge a nominal daily fee. Many coffee shops allow wireless Internet access. If you need immediate access to your emails, stop by one of these local shops:

FEDEX KINKO'S

 187 DARTMOUTH ST.
617-262-6188

MAP 6 E4 1 MIFFLIN PLACE
617-497-0125

TECH SUPERPOWERS – CYBER CAFÉ

 252 NEWBURY ST.
617-267-9716

SMOKING

Smoking is prohibited in all bars, clubs, and restaurants in Massachusetts. That being said, however, there are two standouts that are the last remaining institutions in the city to allow cigar smoking: Cigar Masters on Boylston Street (617-266-4400) and Stanza dei Sigari in the North End (617-227-0295, www.stanzadeisigari.com).

TIPPING

In restaurants, a gratuity of 15 percent for good service and 20 percent for excellent service is standard. For taxis, tip 15-20 percent of the total. In hotels, porters receive the standard $1 per bag; you should leave $1 per day for maid service. Valet tips range $2-3, depending on the quality of service.

DRY CLEANERS

BACK BAY DRY CLEANERS

 145 DARTMOUTH ST.
617-859-2905

HILLSIDE CLEANERS

 49B BRATTLE ST.
617-354-1872

STATEHOUSE CLEANERS

 122 BOWDOIN ST.
617-723-4747

STREET INDEX

OP

QR

S

TRANSIT INDEX

INDEX

NO

P

QRS

TU

VWXYZ

RESTAURANT INDEX

NIGHTLIFE INDEX

SHOPS INDEX

HOTELS INDEX

CONTRIBUTORS TO THE SECOND EDITION

JULIA CLINGER *Introduction, Neighborhoods, A Day in Boston, Shops*

As a Boston-based freelancer and author of the upcoming book *It Happened in Boston*, Julia Clinger has spent the last five years specializing in local venues, attractions, happenings, and history. A graduate of the Iowa Writers Workshop, she plans to finish her novel by the time her children (now a toddler and an infant) are in college.

DEBORAH DUTCHER *Nightlife*

A newcomer to Boston, Deb Dutcher has both a visitor's and resident's knowledge of the city. As a former graphics coordinator for Avalon Publishing, she shot photos for this edition of *Moon Metro Boston* as well as *Moon Metro San Francisco*, and *Moon Handbooks Mexico City*. Deb is currently working as a freelance writer, photographer, designer, and media producer in Boston.

STEPHANIE SCHOROW *Sights, Arts and Leisure*

Stephanie Schorow is a Boston-based freelance writer whose stories have appeared in *The Boston Globe, The Boston Herald, The Improper Bostonian*, and other publications. She has written two books, *Boston on Fire: A History of Fire and Firefighting* and *The Cocoanut Grove Nightclub Fire*.

KELLIE SPEED *Restaurants, Hotels, City Essentials*

A Massachusetts native, Kellie Speed has 15 years of experience working as a restaurant and travel writer. Her byline has appeared in *The Boston Globe, The Boston Herald, Industry* magazine's Boston edition, *Cape Cod Travel Guide*, and several others. She also writes about restaurants and provides chef profiles for *South Shore Living* magazine.

CONTRIBUTORS TO THE FIRST EDITION

Michael Blanding, Alexandra Hall, Jill Harrington, Carolyn Heller, Doug Most

PHOTO CREDITS

page iii L'Espalier, courtesy of L'Espalier; page iii Vessel, courtesy of Vessel; page iii Hotel Commonwealth, courtesy of Hotel Commonwealth; page x The Federalist, courtesy of The Federalist; page x Isabella Stewart Gardner Museum, courtesy of the Isabella Stewart Gardner Museum; page xii Longfellow National Historic Site, courtesy of the National Parks Service; page xii Harvest, courtesty of Harvest; page xiv Harborwalk, courtesy of The Boston Harbor Association; Map 1 USS *Constitution*, courtesy of the U.S. Navy; Map 1 Paul Revere House, courtesy of the Paul Revere House; Map 5 Fenway Park, courtesy of Ballparks of Baseball; Map 6 Longfellow National Historic Site, courtesy of the National Parks Service; page 9 New England Aquarium, courtesy of the New England Aquarium; page 13 Fenway Park, courtesy of Ballparks for Baseball; page 17 Flour Bakery + Café, courtesy of the Flour Bakery + Café; page 17 L'Espalier, courtesy of L'Espalier; page 19 Legal Sea Foods, courtesy of Legal Sea Foods; page 23 Lala Rokh, courtesy of Lala Rokh; page 23 The Paramount, courtesy of The Paramount; page 23 Pierrot Bistrot Française, courtesy of Pierrot Bistrot Française; page 25 Finale, courtesy of Finale; page 27 Flour Bakery + Café, courtesy of Flour Bakery + Café; page 27 L'Espalier, courtesy of L'Espalier; page 29 Sorellina, courtesy of Sorellina; page 29 28 Degrees, courtesy of 28 Degrees; page 32 Rialto, courtesy of Rialto; page 32 Upstairs on the Square, courtesy of Upstairs on the Square; page 37 Felt, courtesy of Felt; page 43 Mint Julep, courtesy of Mint Julep; page 43 Vessel, courtesy of Vessel; page 45 Salumeria Italiana, courtesy of Salumeria Italiana; page 47 Savenor's Market, courtesy of Savenor's Market; page 49 Vessel, courtesy of Vessel; page 52 Vellum, courtesy of Vellum; page 57 L.A. Burdick Chocolate, courtesy of L.A. Burdick; page 58 Mint Julep, courtesy of Mint Julep; page 61 Sports Museum, courtesy of the Sports Museum; page 61 Bernard Toale Gallery, Jump Zone by Heidi Fasnacht, courtesy of the Bernard Toale Gallery; page 63 Gibson House Museum, courtesy of the Gibson House Museum; page 65 Longfellow National Historic Site, courtesy of the National Parks Service; page 69 Boston Lyric Opera, courtesy of the Boston Lyric Opera; page 69 Commonwealth Shakespeare Co., courtesy of the Commonwealth Shakespeare Co.; page 71 Tsai Performance Center, courtesy of Boston University; page 76 Arnold Arboretum, courtesy of the Arnold Arboretum; page 77 Clarendon Square Inn © Stephen Gross 2006; page 77 Hotel Commonwealth, courtesy of Hotel Commonwealth; page 79 XV Beacon © Rick Mandelkorn, Mandelkorn Photography; page 81 Clarendon Square Inn © Stephen Gross 2006; page 82 Hotel Commonwealth, courtesy of Hotel Commonwealth

All other photos by **DEBORAH DUTCHER**

MOON METRO BOSTON
SECOND EDITION

Avalon Travel Publishing
An Imprint of Avalon Publishing Group, Inc.

ISBN-10: 1-56691-974-6
ISBN-13: 978-1-56691-974-6
ISSN: 1545-5297

Editor: Elizabeth McCue
Series Managers: Grace Fujimoto, Erin Raber
Interior Design: Jacob Goolkasian
Map Design: Mike Morgenfeld
Copy Editor: Ellie Behrstock
Production Coordinator: Tabitha Lahr
Graphics Coordinator: Tabitha Lahr
Cartographers: Suzanne Service, Kat Bennett, Albert Angulo
Map Editor: Albert Angulo
Proofreader: Marisa Solís
Fact Checker: Deb Dutcher
Front cover photos: Trinity Church and the John Hancock Tower © Steve Edson Photography/Getty Images
Street Indexer: Andrew Lowder

Printed in China through Colorcraft Ltd., Hong Kong
Printing History
1st edition – 2003
2nd edition – April 2007
5 4 3 2 1

Please send all feedback about this book to:

Moon Metro Boston
Avalon Travel Publishing
1400 65th Street, Suite 250
Emeryville, CA 94608, USA
email: feedback@moon.com
website: www.moon.com

MOON OUTDOORS

MOON LIVING ABROAD

To Lowell
West Medfor
To Fitchburg
Brandeis/
Roberts
Waltham
Waverley
Belmont Center
ALEWIFE
Davis
Porter
Harvard
Centra
Ken
Auburndale
West Newton
Newtonville
To Framingham & Worcester
Washington St
Harvard Ave
BU Central
BU East
BOSTON
COLLEGE
B
Washington
Square
Coolidge
Corner
Kenn
CLEVELAND CIRCLE
C
D
RIVERSIDE
Woodland
Waban
Eliot
Newton Highlands
Newton Centre
Chestnut Hill
Reservoir
Beaconsfield
Brookline Hills
Brookline Village
Longwood
St. Mary's
Fenway
Prudential
Symphony
Northeastern
Museum of Fine Arts
Longwood
Brigham Circle
Roxb
Crossin
HEATH
E
Gre
FORES
To Needham
Highland
Bellevue
Roslindale Village
Hyde Park
Fairmount
Readville
Readville
Endicott
Dedham
Corp. Center
Islington
To Forge Park
Route 128
To Attleboro,
Stoughton, Providence
LEGEND
Terminal Station
Transit Station
Wheelchair
Accessible
Transfer Station
P Parking
Commuter Rail
Connection
Commuter
Rail Service
*Boylston: Accessible for Silver Line Washington Street only.
*State: Blue Line wheelchair access outbound side only. Inbound riders transfer to outbound train at Government Center. Exit State outbound.
Water Transportation Services
F1 Hingham Shipyard to Rowes Wharf, Boston
F2 Quincy to Logan Airport & Long Wharf, Boston
F2H Hull to Logan Airport & Long Wharf, Boston
F4 Charlestown Navy Yard to Long Wharf, Boston
For customer service & travel information call 617-222-3200, 1-800-392-6100, TTY 617-222-5146 or visit the MBTA web site at www.mbta.com
For MBTA Police call 617-222-1212